W9-BZI-662

By Willard F. Harley, Jr.

His Needs, Her Needs
Marriage Insurance
Love Busters

LOVE BUSTERS

Willard F. Harley, Jr.

Fleming H. Revell Company
Tarrytown, New York

Some of the material in this book and its basic principles previously appeared in *Marriage Insurance* by Willard F. Harley, Jr.

Library of Congress Cataloging-in-Publication Data

Harley, Willard F.
    Love busters / Willard F. Harley, Jr.
      p. cm.
    ISBN 0-8007-1673-6
    1. Marriage. 2. Communication in marriage.   3. Man-woman
relationships. I. Title.
HQ734.H2852   1992
646.7'8—dc20   92-15295
                                              CIP

All rights reserved. No part of this publication may be re-
produced, stored in a retrieval system, or transmitted in any
form or by any means—electronic, mechanical, photocopy,
recording, or any other—except for brief quotations in
printed reviews, without the prior permission of the pub-
lisher.

Copyright © 1992 by Willard F. Harley, Jr.
Published by the Fleming H. Revell Company
Tarrytown, New York 10591
Printed in the United States of America

To
Joyce
Together we overcame Love Busters

Contents

Part Two
Resolving Marital Conflicts

Part Three
Recovering From Devastating
Love Busters

Preface

When couples first marry, they think their romantic love will last a lifetime. The vows and commitments they make usually depend on it.

But romantic love is short-lived for most couples. For some it is sustained for only days after the wedding. For others, it lasts months or years before it's gone. But when it goes, marriage and its commitments usually go with it.

Some marriage counselors advise clients to accept the inevitable: Enjoy romantic love while it lasts, but don't expect it to continue forever. Some recommend rising to a higher form of passionless love, while others recommend divorce.

My strategy for saving marriages has been to *restore* romantic love. It works very well, because once romantic love is back in a marriage, people recommit themselves to the care they promised when first married, and thoughts of divorce are ended.

Just as it seems impossible to lose romantic love when you have it, it also seems impossible to restore it once it is lost. Most of my clients don't believe the feeling of love will ever return. But my program does not require faith—it requires action! When clients follow my instructions, romantic love usually returns to end the threat of divorce.

Couples create romantic love by meeting each other's most important emotional needs during courtship. After marriage, habits can develop that destroy their love for each other. I call those destructive habits Love Busters. As long as they are tolerated, it's not possible to sustain romantic love.

The lessons of this book will teach you how to throw the rascals out! I identify the five most important Love Busters and explain how I've been able to help couples overcome them. Once they're overcome, romantic love has free reign in marriage.

This book, along with my previous book, *His Needs, Her Needs,* work well together in helping couples build romantic love that saves marriages. While *Love Busters* will help you avoid *losing* romantic love, *His Needs, Her Needs* will help you build romantic love by teaching you how to meet the most important emotional needs.

I wrote this book to help you sustain one of life's greatest pleasures, romantic love. I also wrote it to help prevent your marriage from failing. I encourage you and your spouse to place great value on the romantic love you share. The strength of your marriage depends on it.

If you have lost romantic love, don't despair. It can be restored to your marriage if you follow my advice. And once it is restored, you'll agree that it is too valuable to ever lose again.

Willard F. Harley, Jr.

1

Have You Lost
Romantic Love?
Would You Like It Back?

Karen was in love with Jim within a month of their first date. He seemed too good to be true—attractive and intelligent, he also shared many of her values. But his thoughtfulness impressed her most. He willingly helped her whenever she had a problem; he changed his plans when they conflicted with hers; he was never rude or argumentative; and in general, he made consideration of her feelings his highest priority. His behavior proved to Karen that he cared for her, and that made her feel very secure.

Jim also loved Karen. From the beginning of their relationship, she made him feel special—she listened attentively to his concerns, re-arranged her schedule to make dates convenient, and showered him with affection. Her consideration of his feelings convinced him that she was meant for him. Within a year, they married.

After the wedding, it wasn't long before Jim felt the financial pressure of a future family. Karen planned to work fewer hours once their children arrived, so his income had to increase to make up the difference. To prepare for it, he decided to work longer hours to advance his career.

With longer working hours, Jim's thoughtfulness eroded. He now expected Karen to solve most of her own problems; he felt she should rearrange her schedule to accommodate his; he was argumentative; and in general, he became inconsiderate. *After all,* he thought, *We're both intelligent adults; she could take her car to the garage just as easily as I could. Why should she expect me to drop everything at work to do something she could do for herself? Am I her slave? Is she a princess?*

At first Karen felt deeply offended by his change of attitude. She cried quite a bit but eventually adjusted to his inconsiderate behavior. She took her car to the shop when it needed repair, developed her own schedule that didn't include Jim, and argued back whenever he was critical.

In the process, her conviction that he cared about her almost disappeared. Her willingness to listen attentively to his problems, rearrange her schedule to accommodate him, and shower him with affection almost disappeared. Though she didn't stop caring for him intentionally, she simply didn't feel like caring for him as much. The "chemistry" of their relationship, romantic love, wasn't what it had been, she noticed.

Jim didn't understand that, while they were dating, his thoughtfulness created her feeling of romantic love for him. His willingness to fix her car, rearrange his schedule, and talk to her respectfully helped build romantic love. That feeling changed when he decided he didn't have time to be considerate. His thoughtlessness destroyed what his thoughtfulness had created.

Karen's loss of romantic love also led her to feel Jim wasn't as physically attractive as he had been. Since he'd gained a little weight, she assumed his loss of body tone was the problem. *If he'd firm up a little, I'd find him more attractive,* she thought. But his losing weight didn't help.

Although she'd enjoyed their sexual relationship in the past, eventually she came to a point where she experienced almost no gratification when they made love. She started feeling used and angry, making love to an increasingly inconsiderate man. Finally she reached a point where it became so disgusting that she couldn't bear to continue.

After a few weeks of sexual abstinence, Jim brought his frustration to her attention. "Karen, don't you think it's about time we made love? I think I've been very patient."

"I'm sorry, Jim. I just haven't been in the mood lately."

What could he say? If you're not in the mood, you're not in the mood!

"What do you think it would take to get you in the mood?"

It was difficult for Jim to broach the subject, and now that he had, Karen was not at all helpful. "I don't know. I've never given it much thought. Lately, I just don't feel like it."

Throughout their short marriage, they rarely shared their innermost feelings with each other, and they tried not to impose their wills on each other. The car-repair incident was "solved" by Karen's taking care of it herself. But their sexual crisis could not be handled so easily. Jim didn't want to make love to Karen unless she was willing, but he wasn't crazy about the idea of abstinence, either. Karen didn't know how to tell him what was bothering her, and part of it she didn't understand herself.

Jim had assumed that once they were married, he could make love to Karen any time he was in the mood. At first, that's the way it had been. It seemed effortless. But now it seemed impossible!

He remembered a proverb from his adolescent years: "Each time you make love in the first year of marriage, put a penny in a jar. If you take one out each time you make love thereafter, you'll find that you'll never empty the jar." Could this really be true?

Jim learned the hard way that Karen's feeling of romantic love was fragile. And without romantic love, a good sexual relationship could not be sustained.

But sex was only one of a host of problems being created by Karen's loss of romantic love. Her willingness to meet *any* of his emotional needs had suffered. She wasn't nearly as affectionate; she didn't talk to him as much; and she preferred being with her own friends. When they did talk, it was often defensive and adversarial. She planned a vacation for herself without inviting him. Sometimes Karen couldn't even remember what it was like being in love with Jim.

Stop the Train, I Want to Get Off!

Jim and Karen's experience is all too common in today's marriages. What starts out as a caring and thoughtful relationship often disintegrates into thoughtlessness. When thoughtlessness appears, romantic love disappears. When romantic love disappears, thoughtlessness increases, and marriage turns into a nightmare.

Some couples suffer through years of lovelessness for the sake of their children or their religious convictions. But all too often, they try to get off the train of their marriage and file for divorce. Unfortunately, the train doesn't stop. It's rushing forward at high speed, and the exit is usually a disaster for the couple and their family.

Since so much personal and familial happiness depends on the success of marriage, you'd think that couples would approach it with a careful plan to insure success. As it turns out, most don't give their marriages much thought until it's too late. About half end in divorce, and most of those that remain are not really successful.

I'd like your marriage to be one of the exceptions. I've written this book to help you build a happy marriage that *stays* happy. If you follow my advice, you're likely to enjoy a lifetime of love. The methods I use have helped thousands of couples turn from marital pain to marital pleasure.

The principles I advocate are not revolutionary—in fact, they're somewhat traditional. But many have been forgotten in a century in which we've become increasingly self-centered, caring more for our own interests than those of others, particularly our spouses'.

You don't have to be the victim of recent social trends. Instead choose a course for your family that will make you the happy exception.

The Love Bank—Repository of Romantic Love

One of the best ways I've found to explain the rise and fall of Jim and Karen's marriage is to introduce you to the Love Bank. It's a concept I created to help those I counsel understand how the feelings of love are created and destroyed.

We're all born with a Love Bank. The people we meet are automatically assigned their own "accounts," and every experience we have with them affects the balances of love units in their accounts. All this goes on inside us throughout our lives, twenty-four hours a day.

When we associate good feelings with people, love units are deposited into their accounts. But bad feelings cause love units to be withdrawn.

Once in a while, our feelings are so good or so bad that many love units can be deposited or withdrawn in a single encounter. Most of the time, however, our feelings are neutral, neither good nor bad, so the accounts of most of the people we know don't change much.

We like people who have moderately high balances and love those with extremely high balances. When withdrawals cause accounts to go into the red, we dislike those people, and we hate people with large negative balances.

The most volatile accounts usually belong to those with whom we've had romantic relationships, because the feelings we experience are more extreme. When things go well, hundreds of love units pour into their accounts, creating the feeling of romantic love. When things go badly, hundreds of love units can be withdrawn. If the balance becomes seriously overdrawn, feelings of hatred may replace the love we felt earlier.

When a married couple's relationship starts a downward slide, the love loss actually gains momentum, and they can come to hate each other more than anyone they've ever known. Love units can be withdrawn almost continually, because every action—even an innocent one—is seen as uncaring and insensitive. Furthermore, since these couples have difficulty avoiding each other, withdrawals continue unabated. The end result is sometimes violence, leading to serious injury or death unless separation or divorce intervenes.

I have counseled both victims and perpetrators of violent attacks, and the difference is often only a matter of strength and opportunity. In many cases, their roles could easily have been reversed, since they hated each other so much.

In most marriages, however, the anger that results from an insolvent love bank takes a more sophisticated form: criticism, defiance, stubbornness, name calling, and other types of rude behavior. It gets the job done, since the purpose of physical, emotional, and verbal violence is all the same—to make the other person miserable. The sad fact is that we're more likely to hurt our spouses than anyone else when our love banks are depleted. What a tragedy!

The secret to romantic love, of course, is to avoid losing love units once they've been deposited. All the best intentions, sincere vows, and honest efforts cannot substitute for a substantial Love Bank account. The love bank determines whom we marry, and it usually determines whether or not we'll be divorced.

If this is really the case—and I have ample evidence it is from the thousands of couples I've counseled—it becomes tremendously important to understand how to control Love Bank accounts—how to avoid withdrawals once substantial deposits have been made.

Love Busters Destroy Romantic Love

Romantic love feels spectacular! It inspires poets, musicians, artists, theologians, philosophers, and hosts of others to try to understand it, explain it, describe it, and experience it. It's just a feeling, but a feeling people need and are willing to do extraordinary things to achieve.

Romantic love is also an incredible motivator—for both good and evil. Political, business, and religious leaders throughout history have thrown away their influence, ethical values, fortunes, and health because of romantic love. But it also motivates married couples to take special care of each other—as long as it lasts. That feature of romantic love, that it doesn't usually last, is what gets marriages into so much trouble. When a marriage loses romantic love, much of the instinctive motivation to show special care and consideration vanishes.

Imagine how difficult it would be for you to be affectionate, reveal personal thoughts and feelings, and make love to someone you don't love. Perhaps as you read this book, you find yourself in that very position. It's an absolute nightmare for most people.

Romantic love inspires people to marry each other because it makes affection and intimacy seem natural and instinctive. But when romantic love fades, and you're still expected to behave romantically, serious instinctive conflicts emerge. You simply don't feel romantic, and without that feeling, it's difficult to meet the romantic needs of your spouse or have your spouse meet yours. You find yourself avoiding such intimate experiences at all costs.

With all this in mind, it makes sense to avoid doing anything that would ruin romantic love. But the habits that destroy romantic love are so instinctive to most couples and pervasive in our society that we often fail to recognize them for what they are: **Love Busters.**

To many, these destructive habits seem inevitable. Their course is so predictable that some have concluded romantic love simply can't last throughout marriage. Some marriage counselors who feel that way encourage couples to stick it out after romantic love is gone for the sake of children, economics, spiritual values, and other considerations. While it's true that divorce leads to disaster from almost every point of view, marriage without romantic love also leads to disaster—emotional disaster.

I don't encourage couples to endure marriage without romantic love. Instead, I encourage them to restore the romantic love they once had for each other. But before they can rebuild love, they must learn to stop destroying it.

Avoiding Love Busters: The Parable of the Net

The Love Bank helps me explain the rise and fall of romantic love. But a parable helps me explain how couples can create a marriage that avoids Love Bank withdrawals. I call it the parable of the net.

Marriage is like a fishing net. Each day a fisherman casts a net, takes the fish caught in the net, and sells them at the market.

Imagine two such fishermen. The first takes his fish from the net every day but lets debris accumulate. Eventually, so much debris is caught in the net that it becomes useless. The fisherman can hardly cast it out of the boat, and when he does, it's almost impossible to retrieve. Finally, in a fit of anger, he cuts the net loose and goes home without it. He's unable to sell fish again until he finds another net.

The second fisherman removes debris every day, along with the fish. Each time he casts his net, it's clean and ready to catch more fish efficiently. As a result, he sells enough fish to support himself and his family.

In this parable, the net represents marriage, and fish are the benefits of marriage. Debris is the way people ruin their marriages with Love Busters.

Bad marriages are like the first fisherman's net. Angry outbursts, disrespectful judgments, annoying behavior, selfish demands, and dishonesty accumulate over time, and the weight of all these Love Busters ruins a couple's willingness and ability to meet each other's emotional needs. Eventually the marriage ends in divorce or emotional separation, with a total loss of marital benefits.

Good marriages are like the second fisherman's net. Love Busters are eliminated as soon as they first appear. The benefits of marriage are secure.

As a couple removes Love Busters, they protect the marriage from the loss of love units—the loss of romantic love. Though this concept is simple to understand, many couples completely overlook it.

Marriages usually go one of two ways: Nature takes its course and eventually love is squandered, or a couple can make a special effort to be considerate and thoughtful by eliminating Love Busters. The second course produces the marriage benefits we had hoped to gain.

Each spouse is his or her mate's most dangerous threat of pain and sorrow. We have unprecedented opportunity to make our spouses miserable. In all too many marriages, that's exactly what happens. When couples come to me with marital problems, my ultimate goal is to restore romantic love. But before I can motivate them to meet each other's needs and start depositing love units, I must first help them eliminate the pain.

How Love Busters Affect the Emotional Stages of Marriage

Love busters not only withdraw love units, they also tend to destroy the opportunity to *deposit* love units. Most people don't want their emotional needs met by someone who hurts them. They automatically throw up an emotional barrier to defend themselves from harmful behavior. But that same barrier also insulates them from considerate behavior. To help couples understand this principle, I divide marriage into three emotional stages.

In the first stage, **Intimacy,** a husband and wife meet each other's most important emotional needs and deposit love units. They engage in few Love Busters and as a result withdraw few love units. This is the way marriage is meant to be.

The second stage is **Conflict.** Here a couple engages in Love Busters, but they haven't drawn emotional barriers to defend themselves from the pain of those habits. Because the barriers are not in place, when emotional needs are met, love units are deposited into each other's love banks.

The third stage is **Withdrawal.** Now the pain of Love Busters causes one or both spouses to create an emotional barrier. The barrier makes those destructive habits less painful, but it prevents positive behavior from penetrating as well.

Couples move from one emotional stage to another during marriage. They generally begin with Intimacy and eventually move to Conflict when Love Busters emerge. During conflict, the effort to overcome one Love Buster can lead to another. But throughout Conflict, the couple is emotionally "wired in." In other words, they're sensitive to the way they affect each other, both positively and negatively.

In some cases, couples overcome Love Busters in the conflict stage and return to Intimacy. But in others, Love Busters are not overcome and grow to be even more destructive. After one or both spouses reach a point of despair, they try to escape the pounding by building an emotional wall between themselves. At that point they are no longer emotionally wired into each other; they have entered the stage of Withdrawal.

The emotional barrier in the Withdrawal stage may be one-sided. In many marriages, the Love Busters come from only one spouse, so the barrier is created only by the other. In this situation, the offending spouse tries to break down the barrier, but the effort only makes matters worse. The spouse who created the barrier becomes increasingly defensive, and the barrier is reinforced.

Once a couple find themselves in the Withdrawal stage, they may try to return to Intimacy from time to time. But once they drop the emotional barrier, they rediscover the Love Busters, and that leads to immediate conflict. All too often, they find the pain so intense that they quickly return to the Withdrawal stage, more discouraged than ever.

When I counsel couples, one or both are usually in the Withdrawal stage. That's why it is almost impossible to begin counseling with an emphasis on *depositing* love units. I must always begin by encouraging them to stop *withdrawing* love units. Only when the threat of pain has been overcome do couples lower their defenses and permit deposits of love units.

Stop the Pain Before the Gain

Romantic love is created by behavior that meets a person's most important emotional needs. The book I wrote to help couples learn to identify and meet these needs is *His Needs, Her Needs* (Revell, 1986).

But there's really no point in learning how to build romantic love if you engage in Love Busters. They will destroy all you try to build. I've written *Love Busters* to teach you and your spouse how to protect yourselves from your own destructive instincts and help you create the climate for meeting emotional needs.

I've divided this book into three parts. The first part introduces the five most common Love Busters and describes how to overcome them.

The second part illustrates how these Love Busters prevent couples from resolving common marital conflicts. Once the Love Busters are overcome, the conflicts are more easily resolved.

The third part of this book introduces Love Busters that are potentially destructive. Even after they've been overcome, most couples have little hope their love will be restored.

But the example of some couples shows us how to resist the overwhelming odds to find romantic love in these difficult situations.

By the time you finish this book, you should be prepared to preserve the love in your marriage—to create a marriage that *stays* romantic and fulfilling. That's when you will be able to benefit from *His Needs, Her Needs,* which will show you how to build romantic love.

Before I begin with the first Love Buster, however, we need a working definition. Throughout the book, I'll use the terms *Love Busters* and *destructive marital habits* interchangeably. Let's define them in terms of what they do:

> **A destructive marital habit, or Love Buster, is repeated behavior of a spouse that causes the other to be unhappy (withdraw love units).**

Any act that makes your spouse unhappy destroys love units. But a *habit* that destroys love units multiplies the damage, because it's repeated over and over. Single acts of inconsideration do not usually destroy romantic love. When such acts are repeated and become predictable, however, love suffers the greatest loss.

My counseling focuses on habits, both good and bad, since habits tend to dominate our everyday behavior. If I can help a couple eliminate harmful habits and develop positive ones, romantic love is restored. When that's achieved, love units are deposited continually and predictably by the caring habits. They're withdrawn only on a random and isolated basis, because uncaring behavior is never allowed to become habitual.

Through years of marriage counseling, I've been made aware of a host of Love Busters. Most of them fall into five categories: angry outbursts, disrespectful judgments, annoying behavior, selfish demands, and dishonesty. Since each category of behavior can destroy romantic love, each deserves special consideration in Part I.

Let Me Emphasize . . .

Marriages usually begin with lots of romantic love, because couples make an effort to meet each other's needs and avoid insensitive and selfish behavior during courtship. Such behavior deposits love units in the Love Bank, and thoughtfulness keeps them from being withdrawn. The result is large Love Bank balances that trigger and sustain romantic love.

But after marriage, the pressures of life often cause couples to become thoughtless. They begin to engage in Love Busters almost from the beginning, and the result is a loss of romantic love. Once that's gone, it usually damages the willingness to meet important emotional needs. With few, if any, love units being deposited and large numbers being withdrawn, couples often find their Love Banks bankrupt.

The pain of Love Busters causes couples to erect emotional barriers to defend themselves. These barriers prevent the loss of love units, but they also prevent deposits. Such couples find themselves in the Withdrawal stage of marriage. When the barriers are dropped but Love Busters remain, they're in the Conflict stage. Only when the Love Busters are removed can they return to Intimacy, where Love Bank deposits are made and withdrawals are avoided.

Many people believe the loss of romantic love in marriage is inevitable. But this book was written to stop the "inevitable." By focusing attention on those habits that withdraw love units, couples will be encouraged to see them for what they are—Love Busters. Once identified and eventually eliminated, these habits will no longer rob marriages of romantic love.

Think It Through

1. What is the Love Bank, and how does it work?
2. How does romantic love motivate us? Why are so many people willing to sacrifice everything for it?
3. Explain the Parable of the Net in your own words.
4. What are the three emotional stages of marriage? Think of examples in your own marriage when you passed through all three stages.
5. How would the lack of romantic love affect your willingness and ability to meet your spouse's emotional needs?
6. What is a Love Buster?

Part One

The Five Love Busters

2

Love Buster #1: Angry Outbursts

Who Wants to Live With a Time Bomb?

Jill's father was kind and generous 99 percent of the time. But during that remaining 1 percent, he terrorized the entire household with his anger. So when her boyfriend, Sam, lost his temper once in a while, she considered him well-mannered, compared to her father's outrageous behavior. Sam didn't hit anybody; he didn't break furniture; and he was never arrested for disorderly conduct: a real gentleman!

Before marriage, Sam's anger was directed away from Jill. He'd be disgusted with other drivers on the road; he'd fume over his boss's foolish decisions; and he'd become irate when salespeople failed to wait on him quickly. Jill did many of the same things, so she chalked it off to human nature.

One morning, soon after they were married, Sam had overslept and was making every effort to avoid being late for work. Jill had also overslept and was also running late. When Sam was about to get dressed, he discovered he had no clean shirts.

Since they both worked, Jill and Sam washed and ironed their own clothes. They'd often do it together but had not yet worked out a division of household responsibilities. It had worked out all right until now. Sam was short on shirts, and he needed someone to blame for his misfortune. Jill was close at hand.

"Jill, I'm out of shirts," he shouted.

She didn't quite know how to respond, so she tried to lighten up the situation. "I don't think any of mine will fit you."

"Was that supposed to be funny?" Sam shot back.

"Wear the one you wore yesterday or wash and iron one."

Jill was trying to be helpful, but Sam had already decided she was at fault.

"You had to notice that I was out of shirts last night."

"Me, notice your shirts? Please get serious." With that she turned to finish getting ready herself.

"I'm not finished talking to you. You knew I was out of shirts, didn't you?"

Jill started to cry. This was the first time Sam had directed his anger toward her. Although he was not being violent, it hurt her deeply. Sam left the room, and nothing more was said of the incident.

This angry outburst was the first of many Jill would endure during the first year of their marriage. The pattern would always be the same: He would lose his temper, blame Jill for his problem, she would cry, and he would back off. As time passed, the frequency of these outbursts increased.

They were planning to have children, but Jill wisely chose to see a marriage counselor first. She was afraid Sam's anger would eventually turn into the mayhem she had witnessed as a child.

She was wise to see a marriage counselor for another reason, too. Sam's minor outbursts were draining her Love Bank. After one year of marriage, she had begun to lose her feeling of romantic love.

Every time Sam became angry with Jill, he was trying to punish her.

She not only suffered from the pain of the punishment itself, but also from the hurt feelings that occurred when the man who was supposed to protect her became a threat.

Why do couples destroy their love with angry outbursts? In most cases, they don't understand what they're doing. One partner thinks it "teaches" the other a lesson, letting that spouse know what it feels like to be hurt. Besides, the angry partner thinks their love will not be affected by the punishment—after all, they promised to love each other forever!

That assumption is wrong. The wedding vows sound hopeful, but the Love Bank decides the issue. When couples deliberately try to hurt each other, they destroy carefully built but fragile Love Bank accounts. Romantic love becomes the victim of their anger.

Anger: A Threat to Your Spouse's Safety

Anger is the feeling that other people cause your unhappiness, and they'll keep upsetting you until they're punished. They can't be reasoned with; the only thing they understand is pain and personal loss. Once you inflict that punishment, they'll think twice about making you unhappy again!

Anger convinces people that the solution to their trouble is to punish the troublemaker. This emotion overrides intelligence, which knows that punishment usually doesn't solve problems; it only makes the people you punish angry and often causes them to want to inflict punishment on you.

When you become angry with your spouse, you have failed to protect your spouse. Anger, which wants you to hurt the one you love, wins out over intelligence, which wants you to provide your spouse safety and security. When anger wins, romantic love loses.

Each of us has our own private arsenal of weapons we can use when we're angry. If we think someone deserves to be punished, we're able to unlock the gate and select an appropriate weapon. Sometimes the weapons are verbal (ridicule and sarcasm), sometimes they're devious plots to cause suffering, and sometimes they're physical. But they all have in common the ability to hurt people. And when we release our anger on our spouses, we can hurt them more than anyone else, because they are the most vulnerable to our anger.

Most of the angry husbands and wives I've counseled have fairly harmless arsenals—like Sam's outbursts. Others are extremely dangerous. Many of my clients have been arrested for physical abuse, and some have spent time in prison for having beaten their spouses. Most are remorseful at first, but after they go through a time of hand wringing, the conversation usually turns to lessons their spouses need to learn. The bottom line for most of these clients is that they feel their spouses deserve their punishment.

When a relationship becomes violent—the extreme form of angry outbursts—there is a good chance that an effort to restore romantic love is too great a risk to the abused partner. My experience working with violent clients has led me to conclude that therapy does not suddenly end abusive acts. When it's successful, the abuse gradually decreases and eventually becomes an uncommon event. When I help a client overcome a tendency to call his spouse a disrespectful name, occasional failures do not threaten the safety of his spouse. But it's quite another matter when the failure takes the form of attempted murder!

I've heard many husbands swear they'll never hit their wives again, only to inflict more bruises and broken bones before therapy has ended. Some men have tried to kill their wives after claiming to be "cured" of violent tendencies in a religious service. One man attempted to kill his wife *three times* before she finally divorced him. He spent time in prison for her attempted murder. Even then, the leaders of her church tried to convince her that she'd sinned by not submitting to his will and giving him another chance! We have countless illustrations of murdered and permanently injured men and women who gave their spouses one chance too many.

But angry outbursts that are not life threatening are very appropriate for therapy. The procedure that leads to success assumes that a certain degree of failure will exist. But over time, this method helps eliminate one of the quickest ways to withdraw love units.

Overcoming Angry Outbursts

The method I use to help couples overcome angry outbursts has two essential parts. First I help them to understand how the emotional reaction of anger dominates their intelligent reaction to provide protection.

Anger is deceitful: It lets you forget what really happened. It is also cunning: It tries to convince your intelligence that anger is a correct and appropriate reaction to disappointment.

But once anger is brought out into the light of day, a couple can see it as the ugly thing that it is. It has no business being in a romantic relationship.

Once a husband and wife discover the ugliness of anger and become willing to crush it, they are ready for the second part of my method: the elimination of angry outbursts. I use a common behavioral strategy that has proven to be very effective. Counselors who have not been trained in behavioral methods often ridicule these methods for their simplicity. But those of us who have seen their effectiveness know there's nothing wrong with a method, just because it's simple.

Step 1: Uncovering the Monster

A couple who have a problem with angry outbursts need to see it for what it is and understand the control it has over them. Sometimes I help them discover its ugliness and control through my conversation with them, and sometimes I use the following questionnaire.

Angry Outbursts Questionnaire

Please answer the following questions. The part of each question that refers to your spouse should reflect your best guess, without your asking your spouse directly for the answer.

1. What are the most important reasons that (A) you direct angry outbursts toward your spouse? (B) Your spouse directs angry outbursts toward you?

(A) _____

(B) _____

2. (A) When you direct angry outbursts toward your spouse, what do you typically do? (B) When your spouse directs angry outbursts toward you, what does he/she typically do?

(A) _____

(B) _____

3. (A) When you direct angry outbursts toward your spouse, what hurts your spouse the most? (B) When your spouse directs angry outbursts toward you, what hurts you the most?

(A) _____

(B) _____

4. (A) When do you try to control angry outbursts toward your spouse and how do you do it? (B) When does your spouse try to control angry outbursts toward you, and how does he/she do it?

(A) _____

(B) _____

5. If you were to decide that you would never direct another angry outburst toward your spouse, would you be able to stop? Why or why not?

6. Are you willing to stop directing angry outbursts toward your spouse? Why or why not?

This questionnaire forces the couple to turn an essentially emotional reaction (anger) into an intelligent decision. Our intelligence usually wants us to protect our spouses from danger and recognizes that the greatest danger comes from within us. Once we've recognized that danger, we're in a better position to do something about it.

This questionnaire, when given to both husband and wife, helps identify the emotional motive for angry outbursts (question 1), their course of action (question 2), their destructiveness (question 3), past efforts to avoid them (question 4), their ability to stop them (question 5), and their willingness to stop them (question 6).

When we answer these questions, we become aware of how our emotions can jerk us around. Anger often tries to hide in forgetfulness—we forget what it was like when we last lost our temper. If we can bring this destructive reaction to the surface, we are able to see it for what it is.

The spouse's perspective on each question is included because those who can't control their tempers often forget details of their angry outbursts. When the husband's and wife's answers are compared, the truth is eventually revealed.

The first question helps the couple understand the motivation for anger. Typical answers involve the idea that there's no other way to react to inconsiderate behavior: "I tried to explain politely that she was annoying me, and that didn't work," or, "He never seems to listen to me unless I get angry."

The most common motive for angry outbursts is that a problem exists that cannot be solved, and an angry reaction is usually part of a plan to solve it. It's not a very intelligent plan, because anger usually creates more problems than it solves. But intelligence didn't come up with the plan: Anger thought of it and tried to pass it off as intelligent.

Anger's plan may have worked better thousands of years ago, when humans had less freedom to negotiate. It may also work today when people are overpowered by dictators and tyrants. But in marriages the world over, past and present, any problems anger solves come at the expense of romantic love.

Clients who have angry outbursts want me to convince their spouses that they could learn to control their tempers if their spouses would be more considerate. True, most of us could control our tempers more easily if people didn't annoy us, but an angry outburst will not solve our problem. It's an inappropriate reaction to annoyances.

If we blame our temper on our spouses, we've lost perspective. Whatever our spouses did to annoy us didn't deserve our reaction. We *must* take personal responsibility for our emotional behavior, and that includes angry outbursts.

The answer to question 2 helps describe the way spouses punish each other when they're angry, and the answer to question 3 helps determine the effectiveness of the punishment. The more effective the punishment, the more love units are lost.

My experience with clients' angry outbursts convinces me that little planning goes into their development. The arsenal of weapons used in anger seems to be instinctive for most of us. Some tend to use profanity and name calling, while others resort to physical means such as throwing objects, slapping, pulling hair, and kicking. Of course, some use all of the above! But whenever an angry outburst is observed, the primitive, childish nature of the behavior usually appears unmistakable.

Since angry outbursts are usually so childish, they not only withdraw love units, they also inspire a profound disrespect—people make complete fools of themselves when they lose their tempers.

A careful study of the answers to questions 2 and 3 provides insight into the destructiveness of these habits. In some cases, the recipient spouse regards the anger as "cute." But in most cases it has its intended effect—it hurts! As a counselor, I focus first on the behavior that does the most damage, and eventually I try to eliminate it all.

Question 4 helps me understand how my clients have tried to control their tempers. This is often helpful, since many could be successful with methods that their spouses prevent them from using. For example, a favorite method is to leave the house to cool off when a discussion is about to lead to an angry outburst. But if a spouse tries to stop the angry partner from leaving, an alternative solution may not be available, and an ugly scene may result.

If a spouse cooperates with the mate's method to avoid angry outbursts, sometimes that solves the problem. In many cases a path of escape is all that's needed.

Can you control your temper? Question 5 helps me determine if anger has the upper hand. Many of the couples I counsel reach that conclusion after one or both have been hurt more than either intended or after they tried to stop and failed.

The final question in my questionnaire is all-important, because without a willingness to control angry outbursts, all sensible approaches to anger reduction are doomed to failure. It's amazing to me how many feel that their anger is their last line of defense, and without it they will be either enslaved or destroyed.

Whenever someone indicates an unwillingness to control angry outbursts, I continue to counsel them individually until they've changed their minds. There's no point in continuing marriage counseling without such willingness.

Some clients fake a willingness to change, to keep their spouses from leaving them. But as we proceed with the second step of this process, their deception is eventually unmasked, and I return them to the point of their unwillingness with individual therapy.

Step 2: Throwing Out the Monster

Once a couple has agreed to overcome angry outbursts, I help them design a strategy to gain control. It's usually based on the client's own efforts and his or her success and failure. But I also use methods that have worked for other clients in similar circumstances.

I begin with an assignment to avoid angry outbursts at all costs. Situations that have led to anger in the past are reviewed, and I have a couple practice avoiding anger while in my office. They can express their feelings, but not in an angry outburst.

Some counselors feel that anger is a good way to express deep emotional feelings, and efforts to suppress anger are unhealthy. But people can learn to express resentment and frustration in a way that's not intended to hurt others. In my counseling sessions, I try to teach couples to explain their feelings without hurting or threatening to hurt each other.

Most couples I counsel learn to avoid angry outbursts almost immediately, and they have little need for a review of progress. But some find anger more difficult to overcome. For these I use the following questionnaire to measure progress:

Angry Outbursts Worksheet

Please list all instances of your spouse's angry outbursts and other acts that you consider punishment for something you did. These include verbal and physical acts of anger and threatened acts of anger toward you, cursing you, and making disrespectful or belittling comments about you.

	Day	Date	Time	Type of Angry Outbursts and Circumstances
1.	____	____	____	_____

The questionnaire continues with a total of nine spaces for acts of anger. Additional sheets are used if necessary.

You'll notice that the victim of angry outbursts, not the spouse who has them, completes the questionnaire. Earlier I mentioned that anger tries to make us forget what it did, so people who have difficulty controlling their anger are not very good at documenting their progress.

In counseling sessions, when they read the Angry Outbursts Worksheet, the offending spouse often thinks the partner is lying. But as the condition improves, memory of the outbursts also improves, and with it comes a willingness to acknowledge failure.

While this procedure can be accomplished without a professional counselor, the problem with an angry spouse's memory and the victim's fear of retaliation makes a third person extremely desirable. A pastor or a friend may be willing to monitor your progress and provide accountability. If that doesn't work, see a professional counselor.

In some cases, I've seen couples every day during the first week of counseling, because of the extent to which anger dominated their relationship. I expect the complete elimination of angry outbursts and tell couples that I will counsel them as often as it takes to see that goal achieved. Since I charge for my services, they have a financial incentive to overcome the problem quickly!

During each session I review the Angry Outbursts Worksheet with them. When there's a failure, I try to help them relive the event so that they know how to succeed next time. They often tell me about close calls and how they used a new approach to overcome the temptation to lose their tempers.

Angry feelings are inevitable. We can't escape them, and we shouldn't deny them. But angry feelings don't have to lead to destructive actions, and the goal of marital therapy is to resolve conflicts without being destructive.

Learn to Have the Patience of Job

One of my favorite examples of how this works comes from a couple I counseled. The husband had been physically abusive; he expressed a willingness to overcome angry outbursts partly because he would go to jail if he didn't gain control of his abusive behavior.

It was early in my career, and I didn't realize that most cases of abuse are bilateral: Both husband and wife are usually abusive. But since he was much stronger, and his abuse was more dangerous, I had overlooked the risk of her abusive behavior.

He took my counsel seriously and committed himself to expressing angry feelings in nonabusive ways.

With his threat of abuse neutralized, his wife went on a rampage. During the first week of counseling, in a fit of anger, she deliberately scratched his newly painted car with a metal chair. She also stole silver dollars from his coin collection and spent them at face value.

But he did not lose his temper. I had convinced him it would be extremely difficult for him to succeed, and he took the challenge. He knew his wife would probably punish him for his past abusive behavior and was prepared to take it. He also felt she could be trying to make him fail, and that made him all the more resolute.

In a session with her, I discovered she had no intention of overcoming her abusive behavior. She was totally unwilling to control her temper. At that point, I changed my procedure for all future clients. Now I insist that *both* husband and wife must be willing to overcome angry outbursts, even when it isn't apparent that one has a problem with anger.

But in their case, in spite of her unwillingness to change, he learned to control his temper. Over a period of weeks, he all but eliminated his angry outbursts in the face of his wife's most outrageous behavior. It's not that he didn't feel anger—but he learned to prevent himself from hurting her.

I have found that, in most cases, spouses do not deliberately upset their mates. They're more like the case of Jill and Sam, where anger fooled Sam into thinking Jill was worthy of punishment. Talking through each incident that arouses anger helps expose its irrationality.

Evidence from the Angry Outburst Worksheet often proves that we make up little stories that give our anger credibility. But once the stories are exposed to the light of day and examined carefully, we become more critical of the storyteller within us. We become more scientific and ask our spouses why they did what they did; then we explain how their behavior affects us. That information helps us formulate a plan in which, through negotiation, we can eliminate annoying behavior.

In some cases, couples completely eliminate angry outbursts after expressing their willingness to change. For others, anger is so instinctive and well-learned from early childhood on that the process of change proves costly and time consuming.

But if your marriage suffers the indignity of angry outbursts, they must be eliminated one way or another if you hope to preserve romantic love. Commit yourself to stop the withdrawal of love units today. You can begin by completing the Angry Outbursts Questionnaire and encouraging your spouse to do the same.

If you both express willingness to end angry outbursts, your problem may end with that commitment. But if you find yourselves losing control, take the next step by finding a mediator who will hold you accountable. Use the Angry Outbursts Worksheet to help you document progress toward complete elimination of this Love Buster.

A clergyman is often a good choice to help as a mediator. But if your problem is particularly difficult to overcome, search for a professional therapist who is trained in treating violent behavior.

The mark of a good therapist is his or her success in treating your problem. After a few sessions, you should see a noticeable improvement in your emotional control. If you fail to see improvement, you should probably find another therapist.

The second Love Buster, disrespectful judgments, is like angry outbursts in many ways but less emotional and more intentional. For that reason, disrespectful judgments can be even more destructive, as we'll see in the next chapter.

Let Me Emphasize . . .

Anger is the feeling that your unhappiness is caused by people who'll keep upsetting you until they're punished: They can't be reasoned with; the only thing they understand is pain and personal loss. Once you inflict that punishment, they'll think twice about making you unhappy again!

Since anger tries to inflict punishment, it withdraws love units every time it's successful. It's *designed* to be a Love Buster.

To avoid angry outbursts and their periodic raid on the Love Bank, I recommend a two-step procedure. The first step uses the Angry Outbursts Questionnaire to help couples see anger for the ugly monster it is. This awareness often leads to a willingness to overcome it.

The second step is the design and execution of a strategy to overcome angry outbursts. Sometimes a simple commitment to gain emotional control is enough to resolve the problem. But when willingness is not enough, I recommend the Angry Outbursts Worksheet to document progress. The victim of anger fills it out, because the perpetrator often fails to remember details of the incident. With progress, these memory failures are overcome as improved control over anger develops.

When a couple working alone cannot overcome angry outbursts, a mediator or qualified therapist can provide accountability. If one therapist is ineffective, others should be consulted until the problem has been overcome.

Don't allow the Love Buster angry outbursts to reside in your marriage. The monster is too great a threat to tolerate.

Think It Through

1. What is an angry outburst? How does it differ from a feeling of anger, resentment, or frustration?
2. Why do angry outbursts withdraw love units, while feelings of anger do not?
3. Explain why anger is essentially irrational. What does it expect to accomplish, and why is that strategy unlikely to succeed?
4. What is the two-step method to overcome angry outbursts?
5. Complete the Angry Outbursts Questionnaire. Do you have a problem with anger? If so, are you willing to throw out the monster?

3

Love Buster #2:
Disrespectful Judgments
Critics Aren't Very Attractive

Linda was raised by parents who worked long hours but never seemed to get ahead. The major cause of their poor income was their lack of education—neither parent graduated from high school. But they also couldn't get ahead financially because of the size of their family—five children! Linda, her three brothers and one sister, and her parents shared a small house and just about everything else throughout her childhood.

After graduating from high school, Linda found a job as a receptionist, which paid enough to support her. So at eighteen she moved away from home, rented an apartment, bought her own car, and felt on top of the world.

Tom, a new executive who worked with Linda, found her very attractive. He was well educated, having earned advanced degrees in both law and business administration. But their educational differences didn't prevent them from falling in love.

Tom eventually met Linda's family and was immediately accepted and respected by them all. Her father felt especially pleased that she would associate with such an intelligent man.

At first, Tom had respect for Linda and her family as well. But as their romance developed, Tom began making critical remarks about decisions made by members of her family. Then he became critical of Linda's decisions. Since he was so well educated, she assumed that in many instances he was correct and she was wrong. Linda enjoyed her time with Tom so much that his rare critical remarks had little negative effect on her love for him.

Before long, they were married, and Linda found herself working with her worst critic, her *husband*. Marriage seemed to change the way Tom reacted to her in the office. He would bring the smallest errors to her attention and coach her on how to improve her posture, telephone delivery, and other office skills.

She became increasingly unhappy in her job and eventually decided to stay at home to prepare for their children. Her income, after taxes, was not enough to make much difference in their standard of living anyway, since Tom earned enough to support them both. Besides, she was raised to value the role of a homemaker and full-time mother.

As soon as she quit her job, she went from the frying pan into the fire. At home Tom became even more critical than he'd been at work. He expected her to develop a high level of homemaking skills and critically evaluated her work each day. Her performance rarely met his standards, and before long she spent the day watching television and sleeping.

Since his lectures on homemaking didn't seem to help, Tom turned his attention to subjects of motivation and ambition. When he came home from work, she had to suffer through Tom's "self-improvement courses." Their discussions became so one-sided that she eventually gave up trying to explain her point of view.

Tom thought he was protecting her from her own mistakes. But in the process, he was making a far greater mistake than all hers put together: He failed to protect her from *himself*. He had become the source of her greatest pain. It caused her to become very depressed, and his lectures drained her love bank—she began to lose her feeling of love for him.

You Think You Know Better?

Have you ever tried to straighten out your spouse? We're all occasionally tempted to do that sort of thing. At the time we think we're doing our spouses a big favor, to lift them from the darkness of their confusion into the light of our "superior perspective." We think that if they would only follow our advice they could avoid many of life's pitfalls.

Yet if we're not careful, our effort to keep our spouses from making mistakes can lead to a much bigger mistake, one that destroys romantic love. The mistake is called *disrespectful judgments*.

A disrespectful judgment occurs whenever someone tries to *impose* a system of values and beliefs on someone else. When one spouse tries to force a point of view on the other, they're just asking for trouble.

Most of us feel that our opinions are correct. When someone expresses an opposing idea, we sometimes feel that their "incorrect" opinion will get them into trouble someday. If that someone is a spouse, we care about that person and want to save that loved one from the consequences of error. At that point, no love units have been lost.

The trouble starts when we think we have the right, and sometimes responsibility, to *impose* our view on our spouses. They will almost invariably regard such imposition as personally threatening, arrogant, rude, and incredibly disrespectful. That's when we lose love units.

It's disrespectful to impose our opinions on our spouses, because when we do, we imply they have poor judgment. If we valued their judgment, we might question our own opinions. It could be that they are right, and we are wrong. At the very least, we would try to understand their position more fully. We would introduce the information that brought us to our opinion and consider the information that convinced our spouses of their opinion.

If we respect our spouses' judgment, we discuss the issue with a willingness to change our own minds. In the process, they might change our minds, or we might change theirs. That's how *respectful persuasion* works.

In marriage, the blending of a husband and a wife's value system is an advantage to both. Each brings wisdom and foolishness to the marriage. By respectfully discussing their beliefs and values, they have the opportunity to create a superior system. But they must approach the task with mutual respect, or the process won't work, and they'll destroy their love for each other.

Tom's Enlightening Experience

When Linda became seriously depressed, Tom finally decided she should have professional help. He came alone to the first session, to determine my competence. After I apparently passed his test, he brought her with him to the second session and wanted to be included in the interview. But I requested that he remain in the waiting room and spoke with Linda alone.

She explained how unpleasant her life had become. She never liked housework in the first place, and now Tom expected her to become a professional home economist. A whole lifetime of housework loomed before her. Raising children no longer appealed to her, because it would only increase the housework she had come to hate. She felt useless and trapped. If that wasn't bad enough, her sexual feelings for Tom had disappeared entirely. Everything he expected of her had become impossible for her to perform. She felt very depressed.

In my session with Tom, I laid out my perspective of the problem as respectfully as I could. I didn't want to make the same mistake he'd made by imposing my view on him. I wanted my counseling to be an example of respectful persuasion.

I explained to him that, in his efforts to help his wife, he'd apparently overlooked her emotional reactions. His advice might have been wise, if Linda's feelings had been taken into account. But because he overlooked her feelings, it was destructive. Her depression was evidence of a flawed approach to self-improvement.

Since he cared a great deal for Linda and wanted her to be healthy and happy, Tom was willing to try my approach to the problem for a few months. If she recovered from her depression, he was willing to continue on the same path.

We focused on the process of joint decision making. Tom had to learn to treat her perspective and feelings with respect. At the same time, Linda needed help in developing a higher regard for her perspective and feelings.

In the process of counseling, Linda learned to be more assertive in expressing herself. I encouraged her to explain her position in emotional ("this position makes me feel more comfortable") as well as logical terms. She also learned to respect other opinions, even though she disagreed.

Over the next few weeks, Linda began to express her feelings and opinions more openly and to negotiate with Tom when he wanted something that did not appeal to her.

It was an eye-opener to Linda. Tom had been in the habit of justifying his decisions with his values and logic. When she told him his decision did not "feel" right to her, he would attack her values and argue that values were more important than feelings. She had bought into his arguments, and when his decisions made her unhappy, she had concluded that something must be wrong with her.

Eventually Linda came to realize that his values were often nothing more than rationalizations of his feelings. She noticed that, if his feelings about something changed, his values changed to accommodate them. His feelings turned out to be more important than he had led her to believe.

I'm not suggesting that values simply serve our emotional predispositions. I am a firm believer in universal values that are true, regardless of how we feel about them. But when people use their values to force us to do something for them, watch out! People often couch their feelings in value statements. They have learned to get their way by appealing to ''truth.''

One of my recent clients would not allow his family to attend the state fair. He told them it was a waste of money but didn't tell them that his fear of crowds kept him from going. His family suspected a double standard when he spent much more money fishing that very same weekend than the fair would have cost.

If he had simply told his family he enjoyed fishing more than the fair, the discussion would have turned to his self-centeredness. But by keeping it to a discussion of values, he ended up having things his way.

Tom and Linda made a successful transition from disrespectful judgments to respectful persuasion. He realized that he'd been forcing his version of morality on Linda. Even if he was right, his method was destroying her and their love for each other.

Today Linda has two children and works part-time as a receptionist, but not in her husband's office! She's made a number of crucial compromises with Tom that have freed her from feeling trapped. For example, the money she earned was used to hire a housekeeper. Tom not only gained a loving wife but he also was enriched by learning to understand and respect Linda's view of the world.

Can a Spouse Ever Be Critical?

Some disrespectful judgments, such as political opinions, don't directly reflect on the character or value of our spouses. When we try to impose these values, we withdraw some love units, because our spouses feel offended that we think so little of their judgment.

But when disrespectful judgments *do* reflect on their character or value, we're really in trouble. Not only do we devalue their judgment, but we also devalue them. Whenever you criticize your spouse, you're in danger of withdrawing many love units.

My wife, Joyce, is a professional vocalist and recording artist. As her career was developing, I wanted to help her in every way I could.

One way I thought I could help was to make suggestions to perfect her performances.

Joyce encouraged me to be critical, because she wanted to improve. Most of my comments were genuinely supportive, since she's quite talented. But whenever I gave her a critical "helpful suggestion," she became visibly upset.

To this day she wants me to honestly evaluate her performances, yet whenever I find fault, I lose love units in her Love Bank. Granted, I don't lose as many as I would if I disrespectfully imposed my standards on her. But any negative comments I make take something away from our relationship.

I've come to the conclusion that lovers should not be each other's critics. I hasten to add that I've always been honest with her and have not given her a false impression of my reaction. But it's one thing to sit back and enjoy a concert as a fan and quite another to view the concert through the eyes of a newspaper critic. I'm definitely her fan.

At this point I can hear you asking, "But what can you do when you know your spouse is making a mistake? Do you just sit back and let the one you love fail?"

The answer is found in respectful persuasion. I'll use an illustration with which most of us can agree: the use of seat belts.

When we see that our spouses are not wearing seat belts, we may simply remind them to buckle up. Amazingly enough, they may resent the reminder. If that's the case, we need to let them make that decision for themselves. Each time we make it for them, they will regard it as an imposition of our values onto them. You may think that if they buckle up each time you remind them, somehow it will eventually become a habit. But that's not the way habits are formed.

We form habits when a good feeling or reward follows behavior. If there's no reward, habits usually don't form. So if we want our spouses to change, they not only need to make that decision for themselves, but the new behavior must be followed by a good feeling. If it's followed by a bad feeling, the behavior will tend to be avoided, even when they've made a decision to change. I may have decided to wear seat belts, but if they make me uncomfortable, it's unlikely I'll develop the habit of wearing them.

Our emotional predispositions determine what feels good and what feels bad. Some of us are born to feel secure when we wear seat belts. Others feel confined. If I want my spouse to develop a habit of wearing her seat belt, I not only need to persuade her of its wisdom, but I also need to discover how wearing it makes her feel.

If she says she likes the feeling, she would probably be willing to have me remind her when she forgets. I wouldn't lose any love units following that strategy, because she would appreciate my concern for her welfare. The good feeling wearing the seat belt would reward the behavior, and it would eventually become a habit.

But if I discover that seat belts make her feel confined, forcing her to wear them will cause me to lose love units, and it'll never get her into the habit of wearing them anyway. A better strategy is to discover a way to make the use of seat belts an emotionally enjoyable experience.

Respectful persuasion tries to find a solution that takes her emotional reactions into account. When I find she is not wearing a seat belt, I shouldn't tell her it's foolish and illegal to drive without seat belts. That's an example of a disrespectful judgment. Instead, I respect her decision to drive without a seat belt, but try to convince her that it's in her best interest to wear one. Then I try to help her discover a way to wear it that makes her feel comfortable. That process does not cause me to lose love units.

When you think your spouse is making a mistake, if you show disrespect for his or her perspective, you're not going to straighten them out, and you'll withdraw love units in the failed effort. A far more effective approach to the problem is to try to understand the emotional basis for your spouse's decisions and respectfully negotiate a resolution that takes emotional reactions into account. At the same time you need to examine your own emotional reactions and understand what makes your values comfortable to you. You'll not only find yourself resolving the problem more often, but you will protect the romantic love in your marriage.

Turning Disrespectful Judgments Into
Respectful Persuasion

Few conversations are more irritating than those in which someone tries to force his opinion on us. *This person seems unable to grasp the value of my perspective,* each of us may think. *Why would I accept his point of view, when he's so insensitive.* On the other hand, when someone makes an effort to understand our perspective before he presents his opinion, we're far more open to an alternative view.

One of a salesperson's first lessons is to understand the need of the prospective buyer before he or she presents a product. Each product is designed to meet a need, but does your prospective buyer have that need? If he doesn't, the salesperson wastes everybody's time.

How often have you been called on the telephone (in the evening) by a telemarketing salesman who wants to sell you a new telephone service? "I'm satisfied with my existing service," you answer, trying to explain that you have no need. But instead of politely ending the conversation, the telemarketer begins to read the sales pitch as if you had not spoken. I react to such an approach by mentally labeling that company as one I will never do business with, even if they wanted to provide me with free telephone service!

If we wish to persuade our spouses to our way of thinking, we must first determine why ours would be an improvement on their way of thinking. If our perspective would make life easier or more successful, then our appeal will be considered seriously. But if it makes our lives easier at their expense, which is often the case, our selfish motives will make our position very weak.

In most cases, we want our spouses to change perspective for selfish reasons. We want something we haven't been getting. Our spouses are somewhat willing to do things for us just because they care for us. But if we want those things done enthusiastically and predictably, our partners must get something out of it, too.

Once we're certain that our perspective truly has the best interest of our spouses at heart, we need to introduce evidence to prove that it's in their best interest as well as ours. Our spouses will usually be willing to try something for a while. But the test must have a limited time period and must require limited effort to work.

To explain this method in more detail, let me introduce three steps to respectful persuasion.

Step 1: Clearly State Your Opinion and the Opinion of Your Spouse

One of the best tests of your understanding of your spouse's opinion is to explain it to his or her satisfaction. Misunderstanding often causes needless arguments. You may find that once you have clearly stated your spouse's opinion, you're not in disagreement after all.

Being able to state your own position clearly is also an important first step. It helps your spouse understand your motives and true objectives. For example, if I want my wife to wear her seat belt, I might tell her that I care about her safety, and it makes me nervous when she drives without it buckled up. This type of explanation helps her understand the emotional reasons behind my opinion.

In response to my concern for her welfare, she may explain to me that she doesn't wear a seat belt because it makes her feel confined and wrinkles her clothes. Explaining her position in emotional terms takes the issue away from philosophical debate. It turns out that she is not opposed to people wearing seat belts. In fact she believes it is a good idea to wear them. But she doesn't feel it's necessary for her to wear them.

In this example, we are not in disagreement over the principle itself. We do disagree over the application of the principle to my spouse's behavior.

Incidentally, most arguments are not rooted in different beliefs but in differing emotional reactions to the application of beliefs. If Joyce feels bad when she wears seat belts, she will tend not to wear them.

If I tell her to wear seat belts, and wearing them makes her feel uncomfortable, I'm causing her to lose love units for me in two different ways: First, people usually don't like to be told what to do, and my forcing her to behave a certain way will almost certainly cause her to have a negative reaction; second, wearing seat belts makes her feel uncomfortable, and I'll be associated with that unpleasant feeling.

If I want to avoid losing love units, *she* must believe that my opinion is in her best interest. I try to achieve that objective in the second step.

Step 2: Explain How Your Opinion Is In Your Spouse's Best Interest

At this point, respectful persuasion often disintegrates into disrespectful judgments. Imagine that I had a conversation with Joyce in which I shouted, "Can't you see how stupid you are when you don't wear seat belts?" Not only is that line of reasoning ineffective in persuading her, the very statement will withdraw love units.

Why do husbands and wives have so much trouble discussing their differences? Because the process can be so unpleasant. Rather than discovering each other's emotional needs and working together toward mutual need satisfaction, they tend to ridicule each other. How long can a disrespectful conversation last before it becomes abusive?

Begin the process of explaining your opinion by showing respect for the opinion of your spouse. You might say, "Even though I don't agree with you, I know you have good reasons for your opinion. But I would like to suggest some other reasons that may change your mind."

Some people have great difficulty making the above statement, because they don't believe their spouses have any good reasons for their opinions. This attitude reveals underlying disrespect. As their spouses try to explain their reasons, each one becomes the subject of ridicule, until they finally keep their opinions to themselves.

Using our seat belt example, I might explain to Joyce how unpleasant her life could become if she were thrown through the windshield. I might also point out her risk of being fined twenty-five dollars if the police stopped her. On a more positive note, I could suggest that, once she had adjusted to a seat belt, she would have greater control over her car and might feel more secure in her seat.

Respectful persuasion never involves an attack on your spouse's defenses. Joyce may disagree with me, saying that some people have been killed because they use seat belts: Sometimes they are unable to unlock the strap to escape a burning automobile. I should accept the reasonableness of her defense. Remember, her initial problem was that seat belts made her feel confined. It's reasonable for her to fear being locked in a burning automobile, unable to escape.

At this point in the discussion, I have tried to explain how my position is in Joyce's best interest, and she has explained that she doesn't agree with me. If I were to attack her explanation, it would probably get me nowhere. Instead, it's more prudent to take another approach: simply ask her to test my opinion for a brief period of time to see if she likes it. This is the third step of respectful persuasion.

Step 3: Suggest a Test of Your Opinion

A final argument in defense of your position is "Try it, you'll like it!"

People often make a big mistake in marital "discussions" when they try to force each other to make a committed change rather than a temporary one. Joyce is not convinced that my opinion is correct for her, so expecting her to make a commitment to my position is ridiculous! But her curiosity and respect for me may encourage her to risk a test of my opinion.

I might suggest to Joyce that she try to wear her seat belt each day for a week and see how she feels about it at the end of the week. In advance of the test, I would explain that habits take time to develop, so if she were comfortable with the first week's test, she might need to extend the test for about three months so that she would develop a habit of wearing a seat belt.

In some situations, a test is not possible. For example, investing all your retirement savings into a new business pretty well commits you to the program, once you make the decision. But most examples of disrespectful judgments that I have encountered as a marriage counselor could have been reformulated to accommodate a test.

Clearly understand the bargain: If your spouse is not comfortable with your position after the test, you may ask for yet another test. But if your spouse feels the first test was sufficient, you agree to drop the subject.

At this point many couples forget the rules for respectful persuasion. The focus of attention is *respectful,* not *persuasion.* If your test is ineffective in persuading your spouse, drop it. You may have another opportunity someday. But at this point you should back off.

If, on the other hand, your test is successful, resist the temptation to force a commitment to your position. If your spouse finds that your opinion works, it will automatically be incorporated into his or her judgment.

If Joyce were to try wearing her seat belt each day for a week and by the end of the week she were to find the experience reasonably comfortable, she would probably be willing to extend the test for three months, as we had originally agreed. The problem would probably take care of itself without further intervention on my part.

But if Joyce did not find that my test worked for her, I would be in no position to insist on another test or, worse yet, try to force my position on her. I may discuss the outcome of the test with her, trying to understand what went wrong, and even ask if she would be willing to try another one. But if she refuses, I should thank her for her willingness to try my first test and leave the subject alone.

Remember, respectful persuasion does nothing that would draw love units from your spouse's love bank. As soon as you do anything that your spouse finds unpleasant, it's no longer respectful persuasion. The entire process must be pleasant and nonthreatening. If you feel you must persuade your spouse at all costs, the cost will be love units, and you will probably fail to persuade. I may be able to force my wife to say she agrees with me, and I may be able to force her to do what I want, but I cannot force her to love me. Only the process of respectful persuasion can protect my account in her Love Bank.

Respectful persuasion is also a two-way street. My spouse has the right to try to influence my judgment just as much as I have the right to influence hers. Technically, she has every right to try to convince me that wearing seat belts is a *bad* idea. Since most of us are convinced we should make a habit of wearing them, it's not a very reasonable illustration. Still, none of us has a corner on truth, and we all can improve our judgments. Being open to the possibility that our loved ones might be right about anything is a critical step toward respectful persuasion.

If I want to persuade my wife, I must be willing to let her persuade me. I must be open to the possibility that she could be right and I could be wrong about any issue we discuss.

Disrespectful Judge or Respectful Persuader?

How can you know if you're a perpetrator of disrespectful judgments? The simplest way to find out is to ask your spouse. If I asked you, you'd not necessarily know how you affect your spouse. You're disrespectful if your spouse thinks you're disrespectful. That's the deciding factor.

I've made up the following questionnaire to help identify this particular Love Buster. If your spouse identifies you as one who makes disrespectful judgments, you'll probably be tempted to make yet another disrespectful judgment and claim that he or she is wrong! Believe me, in this situation your spouse is the best judge by a long shot.

In the event that you feel terribly uncomfortable having your spouse complete the questionnaire, or if your spouse would prefer not to, then do your best to answer the questions *as you think your spouse would.*

Disrespectful Judgments Questionnaire

Circle the number that best represents your feelings about the way your spouse tries to influence your attitudes, beliefs, and behavior. If you circle a number greater than one in any question, try to think of an example that you can share with your spouse and write it on another sheet of paper.

1. Does your spouse ever try to "straighten you out"?

   Almost Never   Sometimes   Much of the Time
   1   2   3   4   5   6   7

2. Does your spouse ever lecture you instead of respectfully discussing issues?

   Almost Never   Sometimes   Much of the Time
   1   2   3   4   5   6   7

3. Does your spouse seem to feel that his or her opinion is superior to yours?

   Almost Never   Sometimes   Much of the Time
   1   2   3   4   5   6   7

4. When you and your spouse discuss an issue, does he or she interrupt you or talk so much it prevents you from having a chance to explain your position?

   Almost Never   Sometimes   Much of the Time
   1   2   3   4   5   6   7

5. Are you afraid to discuss your point of view with your spouse?

   Almost Never   Sometimes   Much of the Time
   1   2   3   4   5   6   7

6. Does your spouse ever ridicule your point of view?

   Almost Never   Sometimes   Much of the Time
   1   2   3   4   5   6   7

The scoring of this questionnaire is simple. Unless all answers are "1," you're probably engaging in disrespectful judgments. Almost all of us are guilty of this from time to time, so don't be alarmed if you get some twos or threes. But if your spouse gave you any fours, fives, sixes, or sevens, you're probably at risk to lose some of the romantic love in your marriage.

Don't make the mistake of winning the battle only to lose the war. An important part of romantic relationships is the support and encouragement lovers show one another. Disrespectful judgments do the opposite. If they have crept into your marriage, make an effort today to eliminate their destructive influence.

Imposing your point of view is bad enough. But when your point of view criticizes your spouse's character or value, you're making the biggest disrespectful judgment of all. Avoid critical generalizations at all costs, if you ever hope to be in a romantic relationship with your spouse.

Let Me Emphasize . . .

A disrespectful judgment occurs whenever we try to impose our systems of values and beliefs on someone else. It is usually personally threatening and causes bitterness and resentment.

Our motives may be entirely pure. We may be forcing our opinions on our spouses only because we think they would suffer if we did not. But regardless of our motives, romantic love is the victim of disrespectful judgments.

It's disrespectful to impose our opinions on our spouses, because when we do, we're implying that they have poor judgment. If we valued their judgment, we might question our own opinions. Perhaps they are right and we are wrong. At the very least, we should try to understand their positions more fully.

A particularly destructive form of disrespectful judgment is personal criticism. When we are critical of our spouses' characters or values, we communicate our feelings of superior judgment and contempt. It's a surefire way to withdraw love units.

The blending of a couple's value systems is mutually advantageous. Each brings both wisdom and foolishness to the marriage. By respectfully discussing beliefs and values, they have the opportunity to create a superior system to what either had before. But they must approach the task with mutual respect.

An alternative to disrespectful judgments that does not destroy love is respectful persuasion. It involves three steps: Clearly state your opinion and the opinion of your spouse; explain why you think your opinion is in your spouse's best interest; and suggest a test of your opinion.

If your plan is ineffective in persuading your spouse, drop the subject. You may have another opportunity someday, but further effort would probably be unpleasant for your spouse.

Remember, respectful persuasion does nothing that would draw love units from your spouse's love bank. As soon as you do anything your spouse finds unpleasant, it's no longer respectful persuasion. The entire process must be pleasant and nonthreatening.

Think It Through

1. What is disrespectful judgment? What are some examples of it?
2. What are critical comments? Why are they particularly destructive?
3. How can you express negative feelings without being disrespectful?
4. What is respectful persuasion? How could you use it to overcome a problem in your marriage?
5. Ask your spouse to complete the Disrespectful Judgments Questionnaire. Have you been engaging in disrespectful judgments? If you have, what steps will you take to overcome them?

4

Love Buster #3:
Annoying Behavior

Don't Be Such a Jerk!

Sharon knew long before she married Mike that some of his habits irritated her; for instance, she didn't like the way he'd sit in a chair. She admired men who sat straight and tall. It gave her the impression that they were alert and attentive. When a man slouched in his chair, it reminded her of certain fat and lazy relatives.

When Mike came home after work, he would almost invariably slouch into a chair to watch television.

"Mike, it really bothers me when you sit like that," she told him when they were newlyweds. "Please sit up in the chair."

Mike straightened up and continued watching television with a better posture, but a few minutes later he slumped back into the same position.

When Sharon returned to the room, she was always very disappointed. "Why do you sit like that, when you know it bothers me?"

Mike would quickly straighten up and say, "Oh, I'm sorry."

"You can't possibly be sorry. You just don't care how I feel."

"Look, Sharon," he'd answer, getting a little irritated. "I've had a hard day at work. Just don't look at me, and you'll feel much better."

Sharon would leave the room in tears, but Mike was too absorbed in TV to notice. At first she felt angry at Mike, but after a while she began to feel she might be wrong.

It's such a small thing, she thought. *He needs to relax after work, and I'm just being selfish to expect him to sit in his chair a certain way.*

So she decided to keep her feelings to herself. Whenever she saw Mike slumped in his chair, it still annoyed her, but she didn't say anything—he simply lost love units.

Sharon never did overcome her reaction to Mike's poor sitting posture. Over the years, every time he sat in his chair, he lost love units. Sharon didn't tell him what was happening to his account in her love bank, because she felt he had a right to sit any way he chose. As time went on, Mike developed other annoying habits, but as with his sitting posture, Sharon felt she had no right to change him.

When they came to see me for counseling, Mike's poor posture had become only one example of many habits that made him an almost constant irritant to Sharon. She could hardly tolerate being with him for more than a few minutes at a time.

Sharon didn't believe in divorce but wanted a separation because she couldn't imagine putting up with him for years to come.

Yet his "bad" habits were all essentially innocent. They all fell into the same category as his sitting posture: eating habits, his tone of voice when he disciplined the children, phrases he overused, and his choice of clothes. None of these habits were "evil" or intentionally destructive. Another woman might not be affected the same way and would be delighted to have him for a husband.

Sharon felt guilty about her reaction to his behavior. But it had become so strong and so negative that she felt she had to leave him, or she'd go crazy.

Why Are We So Annoying?

When was the last time your spouse did something that annoyed you? Last week? Yesterday? An hour ago? This very minute? If you're male, the answer is probably "last week." If you're female, it's more likely to be "this very minute."

For some yet unknown reason, women seem to find men more annoying than men find women. But whether we're male or female, we draw love units from our spouses' love banks every time we do something annoying.

As a marriage counselor, I encourage couples to eliminate annoying behavior from their marriages. It makes sense when you're sitting behind a desk analyzing a failing marriage. Obviously, if they would stop doing things that drive each other to distraction, they'd have a better relationship.

You'd think couples would understand that basic principle. But instead they sit there trying to convince me they should be able to do whatever they please. The objecting spouse should adjust to the annoying behavior. "If Sam loved me, he'd let our cats sleep with us at night." "If Ellen were not so self-centered, she'd encourage me to go bowling with my friends every Thursday."

When *we're* annoyed, we usually consider others inconsiderate, particularly when we've explained how it bothers us and they continue to do it. But when our behavior annoys *others,* we often feel we have a right to persist, and others should learn to adjust.

Part of the reason we're insensitive to the feelings of others is that we don't feel what they feel. As a counselor, I try to help couples become more empathetic—see situations through each other's eyes. But the process is imperfect because we simply cannot fully imagine what it is to be someone else. I often wish I could switch a couple's minds for one day: Joe becomes Jane for a day and Jane becomes Joe. If they could only know what it feels like to experience each other's insensitive behavior, they would be more highly motivated to do whatever it takes to become more considerate.

In *A Christmas Carol,* Scrooge is guided by the ghosts of Christmas into the lives of people he hurt. He witnessed firsthand the effect of his greed on the life of the Cratchit family, particularly Tiny Tim. His exposure to their pain helped transform him into a more caring human being.

I wish we all had "ghosts" that would help us see how we affect others, particularly the ones we care for the most. I think we would tend to respond the way Scrooge did—with greater sensitivity and consideration.

Annoying Habits Are Part of the Problem

I've found it helpful to divide annoying behavior into two categories, habits and activities. If it's repeated without much thought, I call it an annoying habit. If it's usually scheduled and requires thought to complete, I call it an annoying activity. Personal mannerisms such as the way you eat, the way you clean up after yourself, and the way you talk are possible examples of annoying habits. Annoying activities, on the other hand, may include sporting events you attend, your choice of church, and a personal exercise program.

Annoying habits are not necessarily a part of our character or identity. Many of them develop randomly, over time, for trivial reasons. Some parents raise their children to be considerate of people. Others leave the development of habits to chance. Unfortunately, chance is not a considerate teacher, and many people are stuck with spouses who never learned basic social skills.

I've been impressed with how these people can clean up their acts after marriage. The positive influence of their spouses helps them become more socially sensitive. They change their behavior to please their spouses, but it also makes them more acceptable in general.

Some habits are relatively easy to overcome. For example, if a woman is disgusted with her husband's personal hygiene, he can learn, without too much difficulty, to take a shower and wash his hair daily, brush his teeth at least twice a day, wear clean clothes, and be clean shaven.

Other characteristically male habits, like spitting on the sidewalk, using coarse language, and telling offensive jokes, are more difficult to overcome. But once a man commits himself to ridding himself of these habits he can usually avoid them entirely, at least when he's with his wife.

Mike's annoying habits had become a barrier to his effort to meet Sharon's emotional needs. They were so distracting and irritating to her that she didn't want to become affectionate, make love to him, or even talk to him. So he not only lost love units, but the habits also prevented him from depositing love units. Sharon had entered the Withdrawal stage of marriage (*see* Chapter 1 if you need to review the emotional stages of marriage).

When they were first married, Sharon was in the Intimacy stage, because his annoying habits were not painful enough to cause her much distress. But as his habits and her reaction to them increased, she moved to the Conflict stage.

Eventually she concluded that his habits could not be overcome, and she erected emotional barriers, entering the Withdrawal stage. With the barriers up, the habits didn't bother her as much. From time to time, she would "test the waters" and return to the Conflict stage to find Mike's annoying habits still overwhelmingly unpleasant. She would then quickly reerect her emotional barriers and withdraw.

My immediate problem as their counselor was that, as long as Sharon was in the Withdrawal stage, no amount of effort on Mike's part would have any effect. Sexual relations were totally out of the question, and even affection was rebuffed.

The only way I could help Sharon move out of Withdrawal was to encourage Mike to overcome his annoying habits. Any effort to meet her emotional needs before he did that would be premature.

Fortunately for Mike and Sharon, his early success in changing his habits gave her the courage to lower her defenses. Without any encouragement on my part, Sharon began to respond to his efforts to be affectionate.

It wasn't that he didn't know how to meet her emotional needs—he was capable when he had a chance. But his annoying habits had not given him a chance.

Sharon not only responded to his affection, she also became resensitized to any annoying habits. While he had made great progress in improving his posture, eating habits, and tone of voice, when he lapsed into old habits, she became furious.

In the past, she'd suppress her anger and withdraw from Mike. But as so many do when in the Conflict stage, she developed a destructive habit of her own: angry outbursts. Now *she* had a Love Buster to overcome.

No couple can remain permanently in the Intimacy stage. Love Busters sneak into everybody's marriage from time to time. At issue is whether the destructive behavior that leads to the Conflict stage is overcome or whether couples stubbornly encourage it. Encouragement inevitably leads to Withdrawal. Overcoming the Love Buster restores Intimacy.

Mike and Sharon's marriage returned to Intimacy. Mike learned the destructiveness of innocent but annoying habits and wisely overcame them to protect his wife. Eventually, when Sharon slowly lowered her defenses, she encountered no further pain. That enabled Mike to meet her emotional needs, depositing love units and restoring her romantic love.

Annoying Activities, The Other Part of the Problem

Gwen and John had a different problem. What annoyed Gwen the most about her husband was not his habits, but rather his activities. She should have seen it coming. When they were dating he would always choose what they did. Either she joined him, or he'd go without her.

Conflict increased during the first few years of marriage. He wasn't doing anything illegal or immoral—most of the time he played basketball with his friends, fished, attended sporting events, or watched them on television. But Gwen didn't enjoy any of those things.

When they were dating, she enjoyed these activities more than she did after they were married. Her interests simply changed, so eventually she stopped doing them altogether.

"John, why do you insist on doing things I don't like?" she finally asked. "Can't we do things together that I enjoy, too?"

"Like shopping?"

Gwen's face fell, and John knew he'd hurt her feelings.

"I'm sorry, Gwen. I didn't mean to upset you. But we just don't go for the same things. You have your interests, and I have mine. There's nothing wrong with that."

If there was nothing wrong with it, why did it bother Gwen so much? Monday night was football, Wednesday was basketball, and weekends were spent fishing, hunting, or attending sporting events. Whenever he did any of these things, Gwen was annoyed.

While he watched *Monday Night Football,* she would watch another program in their bedroom. She tried to develop an interest in football and watch it with him, but she simply found it too boring. Watching him play basketball on Wednesday wasn't her idea of a great time either. On the weekends, she would join him fishing once in a while, but never hunting. Sometimes she wasn't even invited to some of the sporting events he attended with his friends. His recreational activities simply did not take Gwen's feelings into account, and *that's* what was wrong with them.

John knew Gwen resented his activities, but he did them anyway. He didn't do them to hurt her, but she was hurt nonetheless. He gained at her expense.

When they came to me for counseling, they were still in the conflict stage, but Gwen was well on her way to Withdrawal. She explained that, unless he changed his activities, she would develop her own set of recreational activities, and they would grow apart. She was intelligent enough to see it coming, and she knew herself well enough to know that once she withdrew from the relationship, she might not want to return to the Intimacy stage. In other words, she'd leave him for good.

These were not idle threats. They were accurate reflections of the effect of John's annoying activities on Gwen's Love Bank. She knew that once the love units were depleted, she wouldn't have the motivation to work on the marriage anymore.

As long as Gwen was in the Conflict stage, she was willing to make an effort to overcome the problem. She tried to join him in his activities and encouraged him to join her in others they could both enjoy.

I'm grateful when couples come to see me during the Conflict stage, because then they are much more willing to resolve the problem than when they come in the Withdrawal stage. But getting through to John was a major struggle. He seemed almost addicted to his recreational activities. I could see why Gwen had been almost ready to give up. He seemed more married to sporting events than to her.

I didn't believe there was anything inherently wrong with John's activities. I enjoy every one of them myself and never believed I was doing anything wrong. So trying to explain to John that he must be willing to abandon them all was difficult, to say the least.

It was even more difficult for John to consider the change. We went over and over the fact that what he did wasn't wrong in itself—he hadn't done it to annoy Gwen—but it *did* annoy her. He kept arguing that if she was annoyed, it was her problem. I kept insisting it was *their* problem, and he had to assume responsibility for how his behavior affected her.

The notion that he was partially responsible for her emotional reactions caught him by surprise. He never quite understood how love worked. He thought it had something to do with "chemistry" and that if people were right for each other they'd simply "feel" it. He didn't understand what he had done to build enough love units for Gwen to marry him, and he didn't understand what he was doing now to destroy that love.

But John could see that he was annoying Gwen, and he did care how she felt. Once he understood the connection between his behavior and her feelings and saw how it affected her love for him, he made a commitment to develop new activities that didn't annoy her. To achieve that objective, he learned a new principle that I use to help couples become more thoughtful, the Policy of Joint Agreement.

> ## Policy of Joint Agreement
> ### Never do anything without the enthusiastic agreement of your spouse.

In other words, never gain at your spouse's expense—never win if your spouse will lose. Let your spouse determine whether your plan will be in his or her best interest.

So many couples I've seen have been crippled by their failure to follow this policy. They come to my office with conflicts they've endured for years that could have been solved easily if it were not for their self-centeredness and thoughtlessness.

Thoughtfulness is not only in the best interest of your spouse, it's also in your best interest. You can accomplish your most important objectives by taking the feelings of your spouse into account. But without thoughtfulness, you'll probably fail in those objectives, and you'll never be able to keep romantic love in your marriage.

John modified the Policy of Joint Agreement so that it read, "Never plan an activity that does not have Gwen's enthusiastic support." The rule also applied to her behavior. She could not plan activities he could not enthusiastically support.

At first they couldn't come up with much to do together, but as time passed, their activities became more compatible. Within a few months, they both reported that their relationship was better than ever.

It would be entirely consistent with the policy for John to return eventually to all his previous activities. The deciding factor would be Gwen's enthusiastic support of them. It wasn't a matter of getting her "permission." Instead his thoughtfulness gave her the right to accept or reject his plans. Over time, they learned to become compatible by considering each other's feelings.

Sometimes I don't even mention the possibility of returning to the previously annoying activities, because it is so often the source of new Love Busters. A husband badgers his wife, makes her feel guilty, and tries to bargain with her until she finally gives in and lets him go on his fishing trip. That's not at all what "enthusiastic support" means. It means she has absolutely no reservations, and she would like him to do it.

If Gwen had slipped into the Withdrawal stage, she would have encouraged him to go fishing because she simply wanted him out of her life. So when I talk about enthusiastic support, I'm referring to support while in the stages of Intimacy or Conflict. Along with her encouragement, she must also feel emotionally connected to him and enjoy being with him. Under most circumstances, she would join him on the fishing trip when those conditions are met.

Getting Rid of Annoying Behavior

Annoying habits and activities are Love Busters. They destroy romantic love. Remember the love-buster definition:

> **A destructive marital habit, or Love Buster, is repeated behavior of a spouse that causes the other to be unhappy (withdraw love units).**

A destructive act (one occurrence) is bad enough. But a destructive marital habit is repeated over and over. It is particularly important to overcome it because it multiplies the damage of single acts, withdrawing love units repeatedly and insidiously.

Most of our behavior is habitual. We may think we act spontaneously and originally, but upon closer analysis, we tend to be very predictable. We have the power to change, and we can turn destructive habits into constructive ones if we have a good reason to do so. But once a destructive marital habit is in place, it can spell doom for the relationship. Like a crack in the dam, unless you repair it, it gets bigger and bigger, until all of the water eventually escapes.

Since annoying behavior is more characteristic of men than women, some of my clients have seen it as a male characteristic that women must learn to endure. Men tend to have inherently disgusting habits, they argue, and their favorite activities cannot usually be shared or even understood by most women. For men to abandon their annoying habits and activities places them in submission to women and threatens their essential manliness, they maintain.

My position is that the issue has nothing to do with personal characteristics, manliness, or power struggles. We are dealing with the simple issue of consideration. If a man wants to live with a woman, it makes sense for him to take her feelings into account. I don't ask clients to sacrifice their identities or manliness. I simply want them to avoid gaining pleasure at the expense of their spouses.

Step 1: Make a Commitment

The first step I take in helping couples overcome annoying behavior is to establish agreement that they must become considerate toward each other. Although the will to change is the easiest part of the process and does not in any way guarantee a successful result, it is an essential part of the process. Without the will to change, there's no point in continuing. As evidence of willingness to change, I usually have each individual sign the following agreement, a commitment to avoid inconsiderate behavior:

This Agreement is made this _____day of _____ , 19 __ , between _____ , hereinafter called "husband," and _____ , hereinafter called "wife," whereby it is mutually agreed:

The husband and wife agree to avoid being the cause of each other's pain or discomfort by protecting each other from their annoying habits and activities. They will follow a course of action that identifies their annoying behavior, investigates the motives and causes of the behavior, and eliminates the behavior.

In Witness Whereof, the parties hereto have signed this agreement on the day and year first above written.

_____   _____   _____

Husband's Signature   Wife's Signature   Witness

Step 2: Identify the Love Busters

Once a couple agrees to become more considerate, they must identify annoying habits and activities. To do this, I use this questionnaire:

<u>Annoying Behavior Inventory</u>

Please list habits and activities of your spouse that you find annoying. (1) Name the habit or activity, (2) describe it, (3) indicate the frequency with which it occurs, and (4) use a number from 0 to 10 to indicate how intensely you're annoyed (0 = Not at all annoying, 10 = extremely annoying).

1. Name: _____

2. Description: _____

3. Frequency: _____   4. Intensity: _____

The actual questionnaire allows space for ten different annoying behaviors, and some clients need additional forms! I remember one woman who listed almost 100 habits and activities of her husband that she found annoying. But regardless of the number, I generally begin therapy by focusing on the three that were given the highest intensity ratings. If more than three have the highest rating, I have the offended spouse select the three that are the most important to overcome.

My ultimate goal is to help a couple overcome all significantly annoying behavior, but since each habit is relatively difficult to break, it is foolish to take on too many at one time.

Step 3: Why's the Love Buster There in the First Place?

Once three annoying habits or activities are selected, we're ready for the third step: We need to know why the behavior formed and what's keeping it there. I use the following questionnaire to investigate the background of each behavior.

Annoying Behavior Questionnaire

All the following questions apply to this annoying behavior:

1. When did you begin to engage in this behavior?

2. What are the most important reasons that you began?

3. What are the most important reasons that you engage in this behavior now?

4. When you engage in this behavior, how do you feel?

5. When you engage in this behavior, how does your spouse feel?

6. If you have ever tried to avoid this behavior, how did you do it?

7. If you decided to avoid this behavior entirely, would you be successful?

8. Are you willing to avoid this behavior?

9. Do you have any suggestions that would make the elimination of this behavior more likely?

The purpose of each question is fairly self-explanatory. Not only do I want to understand the background of the behavior, I want the client to think it through as well.

Most spouses engage in annoying behavior because they enjoy the activity. They may give a more philosophical explanation, but deep down they know that it simply feels good to be doing what they do.

For example, some clients explain that jogging, body building, aerobic exercise, and biking are necessary to sustain their health. But they carry their activities to such an extreme that they dominate and interfere with their spouses' lives. The truth is, they enjoy their exercise so much that they can't seem to get enough of it. When their spouses complain, they often refuse to negotiate the issue.

Once in a while, I find a client who engages in annoying activity purely on principle. He or she seems to gain no pleasure but does it with missionary zeal. Then there are people who have compulsive emotional disorders who persist in repetitive activities due to the disorder. But whatever the reason for the annoying activity, my goal is to help the client overcome it or negotiate a compromise that makes it acceptable.

Step 4: Get Rid of It!

It is not possible in the space I have to provide a thorough explanation of how you may overcome each type of behavior. But my experience has shown me that if a client does not gain too much pleasure from their annoying behavior, it is relatively easy to abandon or modify. However, if the pleasure is intense, if the reasons are embedded in their sense of morality, or if the behavior is caused by emotional disorders, overcoming the behavior can be a major project.

Whether the effort is going to be easy or difficult, it's often useful to document your progress. Without such documentation, you may pursue a strategy that simply doesn't work. Set a goal for complete elimination or an agreed-upon modification of the annoying behavior. If the documentation does not show progress, change your strategy. The form I use follows:

Annoying Behavior Worksheet

This worksheet applies to this annoying behavior:

_____

Please list all instances of your spouse's annoying behavior. If your spouse negotiated a compromise with you, indicate whether you found the compromise annoying.

Day	Date	Time	Circumstances
___	___	___	_____

My worksheet provides space to document seven more instances of annoying behavior, and a spouse can complete as many sheets as appropriate.

In completing this form, honesty is essential. All too often, in an effort to encourage their spouse, the annoyed spouse "goes easy" on the mate and underreports annoying incidents. This gives a false impression of success, which can undermine the entire process.

Over a period of several weeks, the frequency of reported failure usually drops to almost zero. Since I often work on three annoying behaviors at a time, attention may shift to one of the three that is more resistant to change. But eventually, all three are usually overcome. At this point another three annoying behaviors can be focused upon, and the process can begin again. Or the couple may decide that the first three were the only ones necessary to change.

I don't consider the behavior overcome until at least three months have passed with no failure. A phenomenon called "spontaneous recovery" can sometimes cause the behavior to mysteriously reappear months or even years after it seemed to end. But in such recurrences, they are no longer well-formed habits and can usually be overcome without much effort.

Here, I've regarded annoying behavior as essentially unintentional. Intentionally annoying behavior usually falls into the category of anger, which we covered in Chapter 2. But whether or not your behavior is intentionally harmful, the outcome is the same if your spouse is harmed—love units are lost. Sometimes it's more difficult to eliminate annoying behavior than angry outbursts or disrespectful judgments, because people feel that their intentions are what matters. That line of thinking can get a marriage into serious trouble.

Replace Love Busters With Love Builders

If you simply eliminate your enjoyable activities and find no replacement, you'll either become very depressed or revert to the activities you left. But if you replace them with activities your spouse can enjoy with you, you win the prize of romantic love.

In Chapter 6 of my book *His Needs, Her Needs,* "Recreational Companionship," I offer suggestions for developing mutually enjoyable recreational activities. Why waste precious time enjoying activities apart from each other, when you could be enjoying them together? Think of the love units you could be depositing!

Marriages usually go one of two ways: Nature takes its course, and marital compatibility is eventually lost, or a couple can decide to remain compatible by eliminating annoying behavior and replacing it with behavior that meets emotional needs. My years of marriage counseling have taught me a very important lesson:

Marital compatibility is *created*.

When couples divorce or separate because they're "incompatible," they've been ineffective in creating compatibility. Very likely they developed interests and activities independently of each other. They weren't thoughtful enough to try to include each other in the most enjoyable moments of their lives.

What a shame. It didn't have to be that way. Their marriage, their family, and in many cases, their happiness could have been saved if only they had used a little thought and consideration.

That doesn't mean giving your spouse a chance to join you in activities *you* find enjoyable. It means searching for activities of *mutual* enjoyment until they're found. It means replacing activities that have come between you with activities that bring you together.

Let Me Emphasize . . .

Men's habits and activities appear to be more annoying to women than vice versa. But both males and females draw love units from their spouses' Love Banks every time their partners do something they find annoying.

We tend to be insensitive to the feelings of others because we simply do not feel what they feel. We're more sensitive to what others are doing to us. When someone annoys us, we usually consider the person inconsiderate, particularly once we explain how it bothers us and they continue the behavior. But when our behavior becomes annoying, we often feel that others should learn to adjust to us.

Usually we develop annoying habits randomly, over time, for trivial reasons. They're not part of our identity. Most parents rid their children of the worst and most annoying of these habits before adulthood. But those that remain can seriously threaten marriage.

Annoying activities are different from habits in that they are usually carefully planned. They often represent the goals and ambitions of an individual who fails to consult his or her spouse. Plans are made that benefit that person at the expense of the spouse, and when that happens, love units are sacrificed.

The effect of annoying habits and activities on marriage is powerful. Because of their continuing negative effect, a spouse will move quickly from the Intimacy stage of marriage to the Conflict stage. With no relief in sight, the spouse is likely to erect an emotional barrier and enter the Withdrawal stage.

Four steps toward eliminating annoying behavior are presented in this chapter: Make a commitment to avoid inconsiderate behavior; identify annoying habits and activities; investigate why they formed and what's keeping them there; and plan a strategy for eliminating or modifying them, with documentation of the outcome.

Annoying activities should be replaced with those both you and your spouse find enjoyable. This is what the creation of compatibility is all about. When couples become incompatible, they've thoughtlessly developed activities and interests independently of each other. They miss a great opportunity to build romantic love and risk its destruction.

Think It Through

1. What is annoying behavior? What is the difference between annoying habits and annoying activities?
2. What is the double standard people tend to use when they annoy others and when others annoy them?
3. Why is a spouse likely to be in the withdrawal stage of marriage because of annoying behavior? What happens to attempts to deposit love units when a spouse is in the withdrawal stage?
4. Identify some of your behavior that annoys your spouse. Ask him or her to complete the Annoying Behavior Inventory. Are you willing to eliminate these barriers to intimacy?
5. In your own words, what is the Policy of Joint Agreement? How does it guide couples toward compatibility? How can you help create greater compatibility in your marriage?

5

Love Buster #4:
Selfish Demands

Slavery Is Not What We Had in Mind

Randy and Jane learned to place demands on each other by watching their parents "solve" problems. Randy would see his mother shout orders to his father, and his father would reluctantly obey. Once in a while, his father would get what he needed by ordering Randy's mother around.

Jane was raised in almost identical circumstances. The fact that both sets of parents were eventually divorced did not prevent their children from falling into the family tradition.

When they were first married, Randy and Jane were very much in love. Their uncomplicated lives and their eagerness to make each other happy made demands uncommon. If Randy wanted something of Jane, he would only have to ask, and she would usually accommodate him. If he sensed any reluctance, he would assume that she would help him later, and he'd withdraw his request. Jane did the same.

But as soon as Christine, their first child, arrived, new responsibilities stretched their ability to care for each other, and they reverted to habits they learned from their parents.

"Randy, would you please help me with the wash? I won't have time to do it today."

"Honey, I'm sorry, but I've absolutely caved in. I'm so tired that I can't think straight."

"What about me? You think I'm well rested? I have an exhausting job, too. You get up right now and help me—or else!"

"Or else what?"

"Do you really want to find out?"

Randy didn't want to discover Jane's punishment, so he got up and did the wash. Besides, he knew Jane was tired, and he didn't blame her for threatening him.

From Jane's perspective, it worked great. All she had to do was demand help, and Randy would respond. Jane's mother sure knew what she was doing!

Over a period of months, whenever Randy felt exhausted from work and unwilling to share household responsibilities in the evening, Jane would simply order him to help. He helped her, but each time she gained at his expense and withdrew a few love units. But worse yet, she was training *him* to use the same Love Buster.

When the children arrive and new responsibilities seem overwhelming and exhausting, one area in marriage that often suffers is sexual fulfillment. Before Christine, Randy and Jane had a very active and satisfying sexual relationship. But after Christine, Jane did not feel like making love as often. She was simply too tired most of the time, and Christine interfered with their privacy.

Randy was finally turned down once too often and decided to use Jane's strategy for sharing household responsibilities. He ordered her to make love to him. Furthermore, he warned her that if she refused, he'd find someone else. She was horrified by his threat and reluctantly consented.

It was not what either of them wanted, but it seemed to solve his problem. When it was over, Jane cried, but Randy was already asleep.

From that day on, their sexual relationship changed. Instead of mutual agreement and satisfaction, they had sex on demand. Whenever Randy insisted on sex, Jane would oblige. She rarely enjoyed it and eventually came to hate it.

Housework on demand withdrew some love units from Randy's love bank. But sex on demand withdrew a gigantic sum of love units from Jane's. It eventually destroyed her feeling of romantic love for Randy.

You Can Have a Slave or a Lover, but Not Both

We've all experienced demands. Our parents made demands on us when we were children; teachers made demands in school; and employers sometimes make demands at work. Most of us didn't like them as children and we still don't.

Demands imply a threat of punishment. "If you refuse me, you'll regret it." In other words, "You may dislike doing what I want, but if you don't do it, I'll see to it that you suffer even greater pain."

People who make demands don't seem to care how those who are supposed to meet the demands feel about it. In fact, it's assumed that they refuse the demand *because* it's unpleasant for them to meet it. Forcing compliance includes the threat of even greater pain.

But it doesn't end there. The threatened spouse often strikes back. Instead of granting the wish, a test of power ensues. If the demanding partner fails to have enough power to follow through with the threat, he or she often receives punishment or at least ridicule. But if power is more equal, a battle rages until one or the other surrenders. In the end, the one meeting the demand will feel deep resentment. If the demand is not met, both spouses feel that emotion.

When a demand is made in marriage, the reluctant spouse usually has a good reason for reluctance. When I ask my wife to do something for me and she refuses, it is because she would be uncomfortable doing it. I may try to force her by convincing her that it's her responsibility.

But even if she's convinced and I get my way, I'm gaining at her expense.

Some might ask, "But what if she lies around the house all day? What if he goes out with his friends every night, leaving me with the kids? What if she makes no effort to do anything for me? What then?"

I'd say you have a serious problem. But *demands* will not solve it. If you force your spouse to meet your needs, it becomes a temporary solution at best, and resentment is sure to be the cost. Either meet each other's needs willingly, from a commitment of mutual care, or do not meet them at all. Threats, lectures, and other forms of manipulation do not build compatibility: They build resentment.

Those who make demands play the zero-sum game—the gains of the winning player equal the losses of the losing player. Since the protection of your spouse's feelings are essential to protecting romantic love, a marriage cannot endure zero-sum games. Unless both you and your spouse win each "game," romantic love will suffer. The Policy of Joint Agreement, "Never do anything without the enthusiastic agreement of your spouse," guards against zero-sum games. It will not let you make selfish demands.

To help couples focus on the danger, I've modified the Policy of Joint Agreement to read as follows:

> ## Do not demand anything of your spouse that causes pain or discomfort.

This rule would have preserved Jane's love for Randy. If he had asked her how she felt about having sex with him on a particular night, she would have told him she was too tired. He would then have withdrawn the request, and none of Jane's love for him would have been lost. They would not have made love that night, but their romantic love would have been secure. And with romantic love, their sexual problem would have been easy to solve.

But Randy demanded sex, and each time he did, Jane loved him less. Eventually, she didn't love him at all and refused to have sex with him. When he threatened to have an affair, she told him to go right ahead. After six months of sexual abstinence, they came to me for counseling.

The Fate of Jane and Randy

Randy had not understood how fragile their love was. He also didn't understand how Jane's love for him made his demands work. When she was in love, she wanted to make him happy, and his demands provided a little extra shove. But once her love was gone, she deeply resented his demands, so she simply refused them.

Once his demands were refused, his threat behind the demand was raised (''I'll find someone else''). When Jane said, ''Go right ahead,'' Randy's next step was to either find another woman for sexual fulfillment or admit his threat was without teeth. He wisely opted for the latter.

It's unpredictable what Jane would have done if Randy had an affair. But it certainly would not have endeared him to her. If his promiscuity restored their sexual relationship, it would have been temporary at best, since it would have withdrawn even more love units from Jane's already depleted Love Bank. Sooner or later she would have hated him so much that she wouldn't have been able to stand the sight of him.

The long-term solution to their crisis was to abandon selfish demands. A year earlier, Randy felt that without demands he would have to adjust to a life of celibacy. But now he could see that his demands had also led to celibacy. There had to be another solution, and he was ready for suggestions.

I reminded him that the best sexual relationship he'd ever had with Jane was not motivated by demands but by love. Once he stopped threatening her and began depositing love units, her love for him would be restored, and his sexual need would be much easier for her to meet.

As we saw in the last chapter, it's common for couples in this situation to be in the Withdrawal stage of marriage, in which emotional defenses do not permit either the deposit or withdrawal of love units. This was certainly Jane's condition, and Randy had to prove that he would not hurt her before she would trust him with her deepest emotions again.

He agreed to eliminate all demands. He would have sex with Jane only when she was enthusiastically willing. It took several months for that day to arrive, because so many love units needed to be redeposited in her Love Bank. But when they started to make love again, it had the quality they'd experienced in the early years of marriage. Eventually the frequency he'd come to expect was restored as well.

A Better Way

Demands serve a short-sighted purpose. They're used by a spouse to force a mate to care when the mate is unwilling. When Randy promised to be faithful to Jane, he assumed that she had agreed to meet his sexual needs. Without such an implicit agreement, why would he have agreed to an exclusive sexual relationship? So when Jane didn't fulfill her "marital obligation," he simply forced her to keep her part of the bargain.

Of course, Jane hadn't said anything about meeting his sexual needs when she took her wedding vow. But even if she had, it would have been foolish to hold her to it, if it meant withdrawing love units. Randy could not afford to sacrifice her romantic love, even if his sexual fulfillment was at risk. He needed to solve his sexual problem in a way that preserved her romantic love.

Habits are formed when behavior is rewarded. The way to encourage your spouse to make love more often is to make lovemaking an enjoyable experience. If lovemaking is unpleasant, your spouse will do the predictable thing—avoid it next time. When your husband or wife is too tired or sick or just not in the mood, you take a big risk by insisting on sex. The next time it will be just that much more difficult to make love.

If sex is unpleasant for your spouse often enough, he or she may refuse to have sex with you altogether. To avoid that unhappy outcome, never demand it! If you've made no demands, and you're dissatisfied with the quantity or quality of your sexual experience, you're ready to make a *thoughtful request*.

Turning Selfish Demands Into Thoughtful Requests

People feel used when you show no consideration for their feelings. Even when they've agreed to help you in return for your help, they can still come away feeling resentful, if you did something that made their effort unpleasant.

So as you consider asking your spouse for help, begin with the question, *How will he or she feel about this?* The best way to find out is to ask:

Step 1: Explain What You Would Like and Ask How Your Spouse Would Feel Fulfilling Your Request

This first step makes all the difference in the world. You have just turned what would have been a selfish demand into a thoughtful request by simply asking how your spouse would feel about it. That's considerate—that's thoughtful.

If you do not ask how your spouse would feel, he or she may feel that you're taking him or her for granted. In many situations, your spouse will agree to help you simply because you asked how it feels. Knowing that you care makes the job more enjoyable.

Now if that was all you had to do, most of us would have given up demands long ago. The second step is much more difficult:

Step 2: If Your Spouse Indicates that the Request Will Be Unpleasant to Fulfill, Withdraw the Request

Thoughtfulness is not just the words you use, but also the action you're willing to take. A thoughtful person is reluctant to accept the help of a friend unless the friend would enjoy helping.

This second step cannot be taken by those who believe their spouses owe them favors, have a responsibility to meet their needs, or must do what they're told.

In counseling some couples, I first must convince them that they do not have the right to make demands on each other. It is not only self-defeating, but immoral. We do not have the right to gain at someone else's expense, and that's what demands are all about.

Being considerate is not just a word game—it means behaving in a way that takes other people's feelings into account. If you suspect that your spouse will find meeting your request unpleasant, you're thoughtless if you persist.

This leaves many people in a quandary. They do not want to be thoughtless, but how will their basic emotional needs be met?

I've encountered a few people who simply refuse to do anything for their spouses unless they're threatened with abandonment or some other punishment. They suffer from a pervasive character disorder that limits their ability to care for others. Even in these cases, demands do not solve the problem for the long term.

Fortunately, in the vast majority of couples I've seen, reciprocal care is instinctive, and demands are unnecessary if requests are made thoughtfully. With this in mind, I encourage couples to take one final step when a request has been rejected and withdrawn:

Step 3: Discuss Alternative Ways Your Spouse Could Help You and Feel Good About It

If your marriage is healthy, your spouse probably wants to help you or meet your needs even when turning down your request. It's the *way* you want your spouse to help that often causes the problem. Unless you present your request thoughtfully, you will not get what you want for the long term.

The long-term solution to your problem is to receive help without even having to ask. In other words, you want your spouse to form the *habit* of helping you. The surest way to help your spouse do that is to be thoughtful.

Thoughtful Requests Build Habits

As I mentioned earlier, most of our behavior is habitual. Further, we form habits when we receive rewards for our behavior. If you do something that is followed by pleasure, you're likely to repeat it again under similar circumstances. On the other hand, if no pleasure follows the behavior—or if pain follows—you're likely to avoid that behavior.

With this in mind, can you see how senseless it is to make selfish demands? You're making it *less likely* that your spouse will care for you in the future. When your spouse reluctantly does what you want, experiencing discomfort in the process, you're cooking your own goose!

On the other hand, if you make a thoughtful request, you set up the necessary conditions for habit formation. When you finally arrive at a way that he or she enjoys helping you or meeting your need, you create a long-term solution to your problem. Because once your spouse acts on your request, the habit begins to form.

Do you want to go through the rest of your life reminding your spouse of everything you want and need? You can avoid all that simply by being thoughtful.

Thoughtfulness is constructive. Selfishness is destructive.

But what do you do if a solution cannot be found? There are reasonable objections to my approach on this subject. Some of my clients are confronted with spouses who have absolutely no willingness to meet one or more of their most basic needs. One of the most common is the one I described earlier in this chapter, unwillingness to make love.

Most men and many women feel that if their spouse refuses to make love, they've violated a basic marital responsibility. How can they avoid demanding something essential to the marriage?

In many cases, after marriage, intercourse becomes almost non-existent, because one spouse cannot enjoy the experience for some reason. Sex may be so unpleasant for one spouse that he or she finally refuses it. That kind of problem is overcome when the mate learns to be considerate in lovemaking and rewards the behavior instead of punishing it.

Sometimes love has been lost due to an accumulation of Love Busters, as in the case of Randy and Jane. When those habits have been eliminated and the intimacy stage of marriage is restored, a fulfilling sexual relationship often returns.

But sometimes people come into marriage uneducated about their own sexual response and simply do not know how to enjoy it. This is particularly true for women with no sexual experience prior to marriage. Their honeymoon is often a nightmare.

While most women eventually discover how to respond sexually to their husbands, many do not. Demands make matters worse. Yet men who marry sexually unresponsive women and women who marry sexually unresponsive men find that they must resolve the problem if their marriage is to survive.

These sexually uneducated individuals must somehow gain sexual understanding. I'm greatly saddened when a couple has endured as many as fifty years of sexual frustration, only to discover that they had the ability to enjoy sex all along. They had simply been ignorant.

If you love your spouse, but have not learned how to respond sexually, you're missing one of life's greatest rewards and keeping your spouse from having sexual fulfillment. Find professional help if your own efforts fail.

Without mutual pleasure, lovemaking will never become the habit you want it to be. You'll ask your spouse for sex the rest of your life, and you'll feel frustrated with the flimsy excuses. But if your sexual relationship is enjoyable, you'll both look for excuses to find privacy together.

Sex, of course, is not the only problem where you may need assistance from a marriage counselor. But before you seek professional help, try to eliminate Love Busters first. You may find that once you stop withdrawing love units, negotiations are much more friendly, and your willingness to help each other overcomes seemingly insurmountable obstacles.

We'll discover more about sexual conflict in Chapter 11. I also discuss sexual fulfillment in Chapter 4 of *His Needs, Her Needs.*

Let Me Emphasize . . .

Demands are a shortsighted way to force people to meet our needs. Knowing that people will not enjoy doing what we want, we insist they do it anyway. If they comply, they won't like it and, as a result, will never be in the habit of helping us.

But demands are also thoughtless. Our gains come at the expense of others: We don't care how they feel as long as we get our way. For that reason, when we make demands of our spouses, we withdraw love units, robbing marriage of romantic love.

The better alternative to selfish demands is thoughtful requests. I recommend three essential steps: Explain what you would like and ask how your spouse would feel fulfilling your request; if your spouse indicates that the request will be unpleasant to fulfill, withdraw the request; discuss alternative ways that your spouse could help you and feel good about it.

Thoughtful requests reward our spouses' efforts on our behalf and help turn the needed behavior into habits. They also have the advantage of creating situations where love units are deposited in our spouses' accounts as our spouses are depositing love units into our Love Bank accounts.

Think It Through

1. Why are demands always selfish?
2. How are habits formed, and why are demands ineffective in forming them?
3. What are the differences between demands and requests? Why are requests more likely to lead to habit formation?
4. What demands have you made in your marriage? Ask your spouse to help you enumerate them.
5. What would happen if you stopped making demands entirely? Try it for a while. Be sure to replace them with thoughtful requests.

6

Love Buster #5:
Dishonesty

There's No Such Thing as a White Lie

When Jennifer was dating Ed, it wasn't difficult to be completely honest with him. They both placed a great deal of value in their ability to express feelings to each other. But they had so many things in common that negative feelings were unusual, and that made honesty much easier. Whenever one disagreed with the other, the difference was minor, and accommodation was almost effortless.

But during their honeymoon, Jennifer was dishonest for the first time in their relationship. She felt deeply offended by the way Ed treated her, and she did not tell him how bad she felt. Instead, she told him she had a terrific time. Love units were lost, and *no adjustment was made to prevent future losses.*

From that day on, Jennifer developed a habit of providing Ed with misinformation about her feelings. His job was hard on her, because he left her alone three nights each week. But she didn't want him to worry about her, so she let him think she felt happy with the arrangement. Their marriage lost more love units.

When they had children, they should have made many adjustments. Neither of them felt satisfied with the way their life was developing. But they thought it was wrong to complain. Each knew the other worked hard and tried to do his or her best. As dishonesty increased, their love units decreased.

Ed found his sexual relationship with Jennifer more and more unfulfilling. But he understood the pressure she was under and how tired she felt when he came home from work late at night. It was not fair for him to expect her to rise to the occasion just because he happened to have a sexual need at the time. So he didn't tell her about his increasing sexual frustration.

It's unfair to Jennifer to say she *never* told Ed how she felt. When he was away three nights a week, she did say on occasion, "I'm feeling lonely."

Ed would react a little defensively, "Well, I don't know how we can pay these bills if I don't work."

Because she didn't pursue the subject, he thought she had solved the problem. But she hadn't solved anything. She simply thought she should not pursue the matter further. She told him how she felt, and if he wanted to do something about it, he would.

Ed also suggested once that they try to improve their sexual relationship, but Jennifer explained that the children made her too tired at night. He dropped the subject, even though the problem still bothered him.

Each felt annoyed by the other's developing habits, yet they failed to clearly communicate those negative feelings to each other. As a result, neither made the necessary adjustments to accommodate each other. Before long, they were losing compatibility.

Honesty Helps You Aim at the Right Target

Most couples do the best they can with the information they have. But their efforts, however sincere, are often misdirected. They aim at the wrong target. Ignorance, not lack of effort, causes their ultimate downfall.

Couples are not only ignorant of methods that can improve their marriages, they are often ignorant of the problems themselves. They deliberately misinform each other as to their feelings, activities, and plans. This not only leads to a withdrawal of love units, when the deception is discovered, it also makes marital conflicts impossible to resolve. As conflicts build, romantic love slips away.

To help couples understand its importance, I've created the Rule of Honesty for Successful Marriages:

The Rule of Honesty

**Reveal to your spouse as much
information about yourself as you know:
your thoughts, feelings, habits, likes,
dislikes, personal history, daily activities,
and plans for the future.**

To help explain this rule, I have broken it down into five parts:

1. *EMOTIONAL HONESTY:* Reveal your emotional reactions, both positive and negative, to the events of your life, particularly to your spouse's behavior.

2. *HISTORICAL HONESTY:* Reveal information about your personal history, particularly events that demonstrate personal weakness or failure.

3. *CURRENT HONESTY:* Reveal information about the events of your day. Provide your spouse with a calendar of your activities, with special emphasis on those that may affect your spouse.

4. *FUTURE HONESTY:* Reveal your thoughts and plans regarding future activities and objectives.

5. *COMPLETE HONESTY:* Do not leave your spouse with a false impression about your thoughts, feelings, habits, likes, dislikes, per-

sonal history, daily activities, or plans for the future. Do not deliberately keep personal information from your spouse.

To some extent this rule seems like motherhood and apple pie. Who would argue that it's *not* a good idea to be honest? But in my years of experience as a marriage counselor, I have constantly struggled with the belief of many clients that dishonesty can be a good idea under certain conditions. Moreover, pastors and counselors themselves often advise dishonesty.

Granted, dishonesty is a good short-term solution to marital conflict. It'll probably get you off the hook for a few days or months. But it's a terrible long-term solution. If you expect to live for the next few years, dishonesty can get you into a great deal of trouble.

Because there are so many out there who *advocate* dishonesty in marriage, I need to build a case for my position.

Let's take a careful look at each of the five parts of this rule, beginning with emotional honesty:

Emotional Honesty

Reveal your emotional reactions, both positive and negative, to the events of your life, particularly to your spouse's behavior.

One of the most important reasons honesty is a basic requirement for a successful marriage is that *it enables a couple to learn to make appropriate adjustments to each other*. Without the facts on the table, an otherwise happy couple can become very unhappy as the events of life turn against them.

The circumstances that led us into a happy marriage are going to change over the years. With that basic understanding, we can then see that a long-term happy marriage requires a considerable number of adjustments on the part of both husband and wife. But those adjustments cannot be made unless both parties honestly explain their feelings to each other. Any complaints on either part need to be taken seriously.

If Jennifer had told Ed how his behavior was affecting her on their honeymoon, for instance, he could have made an adjustment that would accommodate her. If he had told her he was becoming dissatisfied with their sexual relationship, she could have made an adjustment to him.

While some couples may fail to make a successful adjustment after feelings are honestly explained, failure is *guaranteed* when the need for adjustment is *never* communicated.

Jennifer and Ed did explain their frustration to each other once in a while. But because neither immediately gave a positive response, both abandoned further explanations.

This illustrates the importance of persistence. The commitment of honesty does not end when you have reported a feeling. A couple must continue to express honesty to each other until the problem is resolved.

In other words, for honesty to have taken place in this relationship, Jennifer should regularly have confronted her husband with her loneliness, because she was lonely regularly. Ed should have done the same with his sexual frustration.

The commitment to honesty means feelings are openly expressed, whether the problem is resolved or even seems resolvable. Honesty must continue through the resolution of each problem.

As I mentioned earlier, your emotional reactions are a gauge of whether you are making a good adjustment to each other. If you feel good, you need no adjustment. If you feel bad, a change is indicated.

Some people find it difficult to openly express negative reactions. They may fear that their response will be interpreted as criticism. Or they may feel ashamed of their own reactions, telling themselves they should not feel the way they do. They may want unconditional acceptance from their spouses and consider that their negative reactions prove their own inability to be unconditionally accepting. Whatever the reasons, many couples try to avoid expressing negative emotions.

While positive reactions are easier to communicate, many couples have not learned to express these feelings either. This failure misses an important opportunity to *deposit* love units. Whenever you spouse has made you feel good, if you express those feelings clearly and enthusiastically, you'll make your spouse feel good.

Expressing a feeling differs from expressing an opinion. While you should be free to express nonjudgmental opinions, too, feelings are emotional reactions to life, while opinions are attitudes or beliefs. If your spouse does something that bothers you, the correct way to express it is to simply say that it bothers you. If you say your spouse made a mistake, you have made a disrespectful judgment. If you say your spouse should not do it again, you're making a selfish demand. The expression of a feeling should not carry judgmental or demanding baggage with it.

Failure to express negative feelings is a Love Buster because it perpetuates the withdrawal of love units. It prevents a resolution to a marital conflict, because the conflict is not expressed. Negative feelings are not disrespectful judgments, and they're not selfish demands. They simply provide evidence that a couple has not yet achieved a successful marital adjustment. More work is needed.

The first part of the Rule of Honesty, Emotional Honesty, helps us understand the emotional reactions of our spouses. Without those reactions, we're flying in a fog without instruments.

Now we're ready to look at the second part of the rule. This part faces the reality that history often repeats itself.

Historical Honesty

Reveal information about your personal history, particularly events that demonstrate personal weakness or failure.

While many people feel that embarrassing experiences or serious mistakes of the past should be forgotten, most psychologists recognize that these are sometimes signs of present weakness. For example, if someone has ever had an affair, he may be vulnerable to another one. If someone has ever been chemically dependent, he is vulnerable to drugs or alcohol abuse in the future. By expressing past mistakes openly, your spouse can understand your weaknesses, and together you can avoid conditions that tend to create problems for you.

No area of your life should be kept secret. All questions asked by your spouse should be answered fully and completely. Periods of poor adjustment in your past should be given special attention. Those previous conditions should be carefully understood, since problems of the past are commonly problems of the future.

Not only should *you* explain your past to your spouse, but you should encourage your spouse to gather information from those who knew you before. I have encouraged couples who are considering marriage to meet with several significant people from each other's past. It's often a real eye-opener!

I carry this Rule of Honesty about your past all the way to the disclosure of all premarital and extramarital sexual relations. My position is that a husband and a wife *must* confide in each other, regardless of the consequences.

I've had clients argue that if they tell their spouses about mistakes made decades earlier, their spouses will be crushed and never trust them again. Why not just leave that little demon alone?

My answer is that it's not a "little demon." It's an extremely important part of their personal history, and it says something about their character. If you've had an affair in the past, your spouse *shouldn't* trust you—I certainly wouldn't!

But what if you haven't strayed since it happened? What if you've seen a pastor regularly to hold you accountable? Why put your spouse through the agony of a revelation that could ruin your relationship forever?

I'd say you don't give your spouse much credit! Honesty does not drive a spouse insane—*dishonesty* does. People in general and women in particular want to know exactly what their spouses are thinking and feeling. When you hold something back, your spouse tries to guess what it is. If he or she is right, then you must continually lie to cover your tracks. If he or she is wrong, an incorrect understanding of you and your predispositions develops.

Maybe you don't really want to be known for who you are? That's the saddest position of all to be in. You'd rather keep your secret than experience one of life's greatest joys—to be loved and accepted in spite of known weaknesses.

Some counselors have argued that the only reason people reveal past infidelity is because of anger. They are deliberately trying to hurt their spouses with that information. Or they might be doing it to relieve their own guilt at the expense of their spouses' feelings.

While it's true that the spouse usually feels hurt, and vengeance or feelings of guilt motivate some, whenever correct information is revealed, an opportunity for understanding and change is presented. That opportunity is more important than unhealthy motives or momentary unhappiness.

These revelations may need to be made in the presence of a professional counselor to help control the emotional damage. Some spouses have difficulty adjusting to revelations that have been kept secret for years. In many cases, they're reacting to the fact that they'd been lied to all that time.

Some spouses with emotional weaknesses may need personal counseling to help them adjust to the reality of their spouses' past. The saints they thought they married turn out to be not so saintly. But the most negative reactions to truth that I've witnessed have never destroyed a marriage. Dishonesty destroys intimacy, romantic love, and marriages.

We must not only be truthful about the past, but we also need to include the present. This is the third part of the Rule of Honesty:

Current Honesty

Reveal information about the events of your day. Provide your spouse with a calendar of your activities, with special emphasis on those that may affect your spouse.

After six years of marriage, Ed discovered that it was easier to have a sexual relationship with a woman at the office than with Jennifer. As a result, he found Peggy a welcome solution to his sexual frustration. He spent time alone with her several times a week, and their sexual relationship was as fulfilling as he could have ever imagined.

Ed justified this infidelity by assuming he was doing Jennifer a favor by not imposing his sexual requirements upon her. Whenever Jennifer wanted to make love to him, he happily accommodated her, but she didn't feel a sexual need more than two or three times a month.

Ed didn't *want* to share information about his daily activities with Jennifer, since honesty would have ruined any hope of continuing this very satisfying solution. Moreover, the announcement of this relationship would have upset her. He still loved her very much and would not have wanted to put her through the grief of such a disclosure. So to preserve a temporary solution to his problem and to keep Jennifer from experiencing intense emotional pain, he felt that dishonesty was justified.

In good marriages, couples become so interdependent that sharing a daily schedule is essential to their coordination of activities. But in weak marriages, couples are reluctant to provide their schedules, because they are often engaged in an assortment of Love Busters. They may know that their spouses would object to their activities, so they tell themselves, *What they don't know won't hurt them.*

Even when activities are innocent, it's extremely important for your spouse to understand what you do with your time. Be easy to check up on and find in an emergency. Give each other your daily schedules so you can communicate about how you spend your time. Almost everything you do will affect your spouse. Therefore, it is important to explain what you do each day.

If Jennifer and Ed had established a habit of exchanging daily information early in their marriage, his affair would have been almost impossible to arrange. In fact, if they had practiced the rule of honesty, his problem would probably not even have existed.

Honesty is a terrific way to protect your spouse from potentially damaging activities. By knowing that you'll be telling your spouse what you've been up to, you're far less likely to get either of you into trouble.

This idea of accounting for your time is expanded in the fourth part of the Rule of Honesty:

Future Honesty

Reveal your thoughts and plans regarding future activities and objectives.

After having made such a big issue of revealing past indiscretions, you can imagine how I feel about revealing future plans. They're *much* easier to discuss with your spouse, yet many couples make plans independently of each other.

Some couples don't explain their plans because they don't want to change them, even if their spouses express negative reactions. They feel that explaining a future plan may ''prepare the evening for war,'' and their spouses will successfully scuttle the plan.

Some don't explain their future plans because they don't think their spouses would be interested. There's nothing upsetting about the plan, so there'd be no point in revealing it.

But even if your plans are innocent, when you fail to tell your spouse your future plans, you're engaging in a Love Buster. It's destructive because you don't really know what your spouse's reaction will be, and by failing to give advance notice, you may create a problem for the future.

The Policy of Joint Agreement, *Never do anything without the enthusiastic agreement of your spouse,* is certainly relevant in discussions of your future plans. It just makes sense to follow the rule, when you make your plans, if you want to deposit love units and avoid withdrawing them.

You may feel your plans are best for both you and your spouse.

Once your spouse sees the plan succeed, he or she will be be grateful that you went ahead with it.

Or you may feel that if you wait for your spouse's approval, you'll never accomplish anything. Perhaps your wife is so conservative that if you wait for her approval, you think you'll miss every opportunity that comes your way.

Regardless of how you feel about revealing your plans, failure to do so is a Love Buster because you deliberately leave your spouse in the dark. While no love units are withdrawn at the time you're deceitful, they're almost sure to be withdrawn when your spouse realizes you've held back information. It also sets up the loss of more love units when your plan fails to take your spouse's feelings into account.

This brings us to the final part of the Rule of Honesty:

Complete Honesty

Do not leave your spouse with a false impression about your thoughts, feelings, habits, likes, dislikes, personal history, daily activities, or plans for the future. Do not deliberately keep personal information from your spouse.

It goes without saying: False impressions are just as deceitful as outright lies! The purpose of honesty is having the facts in front you. Without them, you'll fail to solve the simplest marital problems. Why should it make a difference how you fail to reveal the facts to each other, whether by lies or by giving false impressions? Either one will leave your spouse ignorant.

I need to ask probing questions during premarital counseling. I know the categories where people tend to leave false impressions and search in each of these areas for truth. Since most marital problems originate with serious misconceptions, I do what I can to dig out these little weeds that eventually choke the plant.

In most marriages, the biggest false impression is that your spouse is doing a good job meeting your needs. The truth is that in some areas you may be very dissatisfied.

No one ever wants to be told they're failing at something, so your expression of dissatisfaction carries the risk of withdrawing love units. But if it's expressed in a nonthreatening, nonjudgmental way, you minimize the risk.

The alternative to expressing dissatisfaction is to leave your spouse with a false impression. Either way you'll lose love units. But only the truthful expression of your feelings will create an opportunity to stop future losses. Only the truth can lead you to a solution. Deception can only lead to continuing misery. You *cripple* your spouse when you fail to reveal the truth. You deliver a map that leads nowhere.

Redefining Love Busters

If we look closely at our definition of Love Busters, honesty could be included as one of them, since it can withdraw love units. If your expression of honesty causes your spouse to become unhappy, is that a Love Buster?

No, it's not, because the only alternative, dishonesty, eventually causes even more unhappiness. So to be consistent, we need to modify our definition of Love Busters to accommodate this problem.

> **A destructive marital habit, or Love Buster, is repeated behavior of a spouse that causes the other to be unhappy (withdraw love units).**
>
> **Honesty is not a Love Buster, because the only alternative, dishonesty, is even more destructive.**

As I mentioned earlier, it's extremely important to understand the difference between honesty and disrespectful judgments or selfish demands.

To express my unhappiness is honesty, but to criticize my spouse for failure and tell her what she should do about it is judgmental and demanding. There's an important but fine line between honest expressions and critical or demanding expressions.

"I'd like to spend more time with you" is an honest feeling.

"I become upset when I'm left alone at night" is an honest feeling.

"I'm the least important person in your life. You'd rather be with anyone else but me" is a disrespectful judgment.

"If you don't start spending more time with me soon, I'll find someone else to spend time with" is a selfish demand.

Some who are aware of the problem simply choose dishonesty to avoid being judgmental or demanding. But since that strategy ultimately destroys a marriage, it's critical for spouses to learn to eliminate judgments and demands from otherwise honest expressions of feeling.

If you're not sure which is which, ask your spouse. He or she knows the difference between your honest and destructive expressions.

Let Me Emphasize . . .

Couples often form the habit of deliberately misinforming each other about their feelings, activities, and plans. When it's discovered, this misinformation not only leads to a withdrawal of love units but also makes marital conflicts impossible to resolve.

My basic Rule of Honesty is as follows: Reveal to your spouse as much information about yourself as you know: your thoughts, feelings, habits, likes, dislikes, personal history, daily activities, and plans for the future.

Honesty *can* sometimes lead to a withdrawal of love units. But the alternative, dishonesty, not only withdraws love units, but it also destroys the opportunity to solve important marital problems. Without accurate facts about emotions, personal history, current activities, and plans for the future, successful marital adjustment becomes impossible.

With this in mind, we need to revise our definition of Love Busters by exempting honesty as a potential Love Buster; the only alternative, dishonesty, is the real Love Buster, because it causes much more unhappiness.

The Policy of Joint Agreement helps create a process of marital conflict resolution in which thoughtfulness is the rule: Never do anything without the enthusiastic agreement of your spouse.

Love busters make it almost impossible to resolve conflicts in marriage. Angry outbursts, disrespectful judgments, annoying behavior, selfish demands, and dishonesty work together to keep conflict brewing. This is because Love Busters are thoughtless—they fail to take the spouse's interests into account.

Conflicts are resolved only when the interests of *both* parties are taken into account. The Policy of Joint Agreement is the key to solving marital conflicts. If you and your spouse enthusiastically agree to a solution, you're on the right track. If you cannot agree, continue negotiating.

Every week I see couples who have endured conflict for years because they failed to apply this policy. Their thoughtlessness has not only ruined romantic love, it has also kept them from solving the simplest problems.

That's why thoughtfulness is not only in the best interest of your spouse, it's also in your best interest. You can accomplish your most important objectives *and* strengthen romantic love by taking the feelings of your spouse into account.

In the remaining chapters, we'll discuss some of the most common conflicts in marriage. I'll show you how Love Busters have made these conflicts impossible to solve; then I'll show you how eliminating Love Busters and applying the Policy of Joint Agreement to the conflicts makes their solutions possible.

Think It Through

1. How does dishonesty withdraw love units? How does it prevent couples from solving marital problems?

2. How can the honest expression of emotions be confused with the Love Busters, disrespectful judgments, and selfish demands? How can you know when you've crossed the line from honesty to Love Busters?

3. Why should past weaknesses and failures be revealed to your spouse?

4. Do you share your daily schedule with your spouse? Do you engage in any activities that would annoy your spouse, if they were known?

5. How does the Policy of Joint Agreement apply to future honesty? Do you give your spouse an opportunity to review your schedule *before* you make commitments?

Part Two

Resolving Marital Conflicts

7

Resolving Conflicts Over Friends and Relatives

Many parents make the sad mistake of not letting go. But their habit of dictating their child's every move can devastate the child's marriage.

Shortly after the wedding, Ellen told John that in order to keep peace in her family he must join Trinity Church, where her parents attended. Having been a member of Saint Paul Community Church all his life, he preferred continuing to attend there. Besides, he and Ellen had attended his church together before their wedding, and she loved it. But Ellen insisted, so he agreed.

For about a year, John attended Trinity with Ellen but was never able to make the adjustment. He complained to her all year about how unfair it was that her parents decided what church they attended.

One day he'd had it. "Ellen, I just can't do it anymore. I will not attend a church just to make your parents happy."

"Well, then do it to make me happy."

"But I'm not comfortable at that church. Besides, you always enjoyed being at my church before we were married. What's so bad about it now?''

"John, I enjoy the services at your church, but I can't disappoint my parents.''

"You *can't* disappoint your parents, but you *can* disappoint me, right?''

When the couple saw me for counseling, I pointed out to Ellen that she'd been making a selfish demand, gaining peace with her parents at the expense of her husband's feelings. She knew he did not enjoy the church services, yet she forced him to attend so she would not have to deal with her parents' rejection.

John had made the correct response to her demand: He rejected it. He told her he would not continue to do something that made him uncomfortable. They needed to find a solution that would satisfy them both, and his attending Trinity was not it.

The concept of selfish demands was like a breath of fresh air for Ellen. She had struggled with the issue of whom to please, John or her parents, ever since they'd married. Now she saw that whenever she tried to force John to do something for her parents it was just as selfish as if she were doing it for herself. I pointed out to her that in a sense she *was* doing it for herself.

She felt as if she'd had a heavy burden lifted from her shoulders. They had already attended several other churches and discussed these alternatives. None of them would have pleased her parents, but with their new perspective they moved beyond that problem. Now they were simply looking for a church they would both enjoy.

After lengthy discussions, they agreed that they enjoyed and bene-fited most from the services at Saint Paul Community and should return to that church. Ellen was very happy with the outcome.

When told of their decision, Ellen's parents announced that they would not speak to either of them until they changed their minds. Ellen had experienced this reaction in the past, because her family was into demands and intimidation. But this time she didn't buckle under the pressure. She and John decided to honor her parents' request for silence. It took two full years, but her parents finally broke the silence and admitted they'd made a mistake.

John and Ellen's solution to the problem met the conditions of the Policy of Joint Agreement. They both rejected other solutions until they had each other's enthusiastic support for one. Their final solution deposited love units into both Love Banks, and protected their romantic love.

In the end, Ellen's parents adjusted to their decision. But even if they had not, the decision would have been correct. As their counselor, I witnessed a noticeable improvement in the love John and Ellen felt for each other, and their entire family benefited.

Taking Generosity One Step Too Far

Judy had always been generous. That's one of the traits that attracted Bill to her. But after their marriage he began to feel drained by her generosity. While she had never earned much money, he had. That's one of the traits that attracted her to him!

"We can't support your sister and brother-in-law, Judy. He'll have to find a job, just like everyone else."

"But he's tried, and if we don't help, who will? Please, Bill," she begged, "let's help them just one more time."

They did help. But it wasn't just that time, it was many times thereafter. Eventually Judy's sister and brother-in-law moved into their house—and remained for five years. Both couples had a child during that time, which put an even greater strain on the situation.

When it is wrong to be generous? It's when you impose the cost of your generosity on someone else. It would have been one thing for both Judy and Bill to have agreed to be generous, but it was quite another for Judy to be generous at Bill's expense.

Judy enjoyed giving to her sister, so she did it whenever she had an opportunity. But as soon as Bill found out, he became furious. They had trouble paying their own bills, and when she gave away his monthly earnings, she put Bill under needless financial pressure. Her habit of generosity annoyed him. It was a Love Buster.

When Judy insisted on inviting her sister and brother-in-law to live with them, she made a selfish demand. Bill came home one day to find them ready to move in. She didn't ask if it was okay with him or give him the choice of no for an answer. It was a terrible invasion of their privacy, since they had an extremely difficult time arranging any time to be alone.

Again and again Bill tried to convince Judy that her relatives should leave, but she remained resolute. "I can't do that to my sister. You'll have to understand."

Bill may have tried to understand, but Judy's love units in his Love Bank kept drifting away until there were none left to withdraw. At that point, he could no longer tolerate the situation. Even though it meant leaving his child, whom he loved dearly, he felt he had to go.

Bill's decision brought them to me for counseling. I persuaded Judy to consider the effect of her generosity on her family. First she came to realize her own child suffered. Then, and more important, she acknowledged that Bill had suffered from her generosity.

The tenacity of Judy's effort to keep her sister's family at home with her amazed me. Even though Bill had moved out, she made every effort to resolve the conflict in a way that would keep her sister with her. As the counseling continued, Judy became more obviously selfish. She wanted her sister to be with her at all costs. Her handouts made her sister dependent on her, and that's how she wanted it.

Judy could see the wisdom of making joint decisions with Bill but had a very difficult time applying it to her own choices. She had been generous with Bill's money and effort, but she had not been generous toward Bill.

In the end, the realization that Bill would not put up with her Love Busters saved the day. She eventually chose to take Bill's feelings into account, because he would not come back if she did not.

She decided to become thoughtful and in the process created the conditions for Bill's love to return. Eventually, her thoughtfulness toward him became firmly established, and they shared romantic love for each other.

Judy continued to be generous, but not at Bill's expense. She discussed each generous act with him and waited for his enthusiastic support before she went ahead with it.

I've counseled many individuals who complain of severe depression. After I've had an opportunity to get to know them, I often find that they've been forced by their spouses to endure unpleasant life-styles. In an effort to please their loved ones, they agree to unbearable circumstances that eventually lead to depression. Once the unpleasant life-style is changed, their depression lifts.

My emphasis on the word *enthusiastic* in the Policy of Joint Agreement helps eliminate solutions that might lead to depression. Remember, only enthusiastic support for a solution deposits love units. Certain personality types willingly endure pain in an effort to please others. They are willing to do things that can actually cause a withdrawal of love units. If you're married to one of these individuals, don't let your husband or wife do it. Wait for enthusiastic support before you carry out your plan, or their romantic love for you will be at risk.

The Former Lover

When Sue asked Jack, her new husband, to have dinner with Sam, her former lover, Jack was dumbfounded.

"Have dinner with Sam? Are you crazy? He's the last person in the world I'd ever want to see," Jack complained.

But Sue's persistence paid off—for her. Jack reluctantly agreed to dine with Sam and Sue. She simply wanted to maintain a friendship with Sam and didn't want it to be behind Jack's back. That made sense to her.

Sue felt that Jack would eventually adjust to her friendship with Sam. But as you might expect, he didn't. Jack's memory of her selfish demand became the single most damaging event of their marriage. He never did get over it. But that's not where it ended.

Over the years, Sue continued to see Sam from time to time, and she'd always tell Jack about it. He always became upset whenever she told him, but it wasn't the honesty that withdrew love units, it was her persistence in an annoying activity.

It seems obvious to me that a former lover wouldn't be welcome in a marriage. But I guess if it were *my* former lover, it wouldn't be so obvious to me. What should have been obvious was that Sue enjoyed her friendship with Sam at Jack's expense. It was a Love Buster, and it violated the Policy of Joint Agreement.

Sue felt she had the right to see whomever she pleased. Marriage, she believed, should not restrain her basic personal freedoms.

Her indulgence in activities that benefited her at Jack's emotional expense eventually took its toll on him. Jack gradually lost his feeling of romantic love toward Sue. When that happened, he began to engage in disrespectful judgments by being critical and rude toward her. Of course, that withdrew love units from her love bank, and by the time they came to see me, they hated each other.

Keeping a couple like this together takes the strength of Samson. I first encouraged Jack to eliminate his critical and rude behavior. It was out of character for him to be that way, and he followed my recommendation without much difficulty.

Then Sue came to understand how her "freedom" had hurt Jack. She eventually apologized for what she had put Jack through and stopped seeing Sam.

The recovery of their romantic love was a long and difficult process, one they could have avoided if they had protected each other from Love Busters when they were first married. Their ability to meet each other's emotional needs had never been a problem, but their destructive habits prevented that potential from being realized. Once they were eliminated, slowly but surely Sue and Jack allowed each other to meet their emotional needs and restore their Love Bank balances.

Now they both understand and apply the Policy of Joint Agreement. Each time they have a conflict, they wait until they can both express enthusiasm for the solution. With each solution, they build romantic love.

"I Just Don't Like Her!"

Craig and Joan could not understand how to get around the problem. He knew there was really nothing wrong with her friend, Bev, but she annoyed him. In fact he felt annoyed whenever Joan talked to Bev on the telephone.

Craig believed Joan should be able to freely choose her friends, and she had known Bev long before she met him. He didn't want to break up that friendship.

They came to me for counseling because Joan thought Craig was crazy. "Maybe you could straighten him out," she said, "and then he'd be normal and like Bev."

Even Craig thought he might be crazy. Crazy or not, he just didn't like Bev.

I helped them recognize Joan's friendship with Bev as an annoying activity. It was innocent, as most annoying activities are, but it was a Love Buster. Each time Joan saw Bev, love units were withdrawn from Craig's love bank. The friendship was not worth the risk of losing romantic love.

Craig had no choice in the matter. His emotional reactions to Bev were strongly negative and consistent. He tried to like Bev, but it didn't work. Compromises had been attempted, but to no avail. In the end, it became apparent that Bev had to go.

Every one of us knows someone whom we dislike. I can't believe that Will Rogers wasn't annoyed by *someone!* It's normal to like some people and dislike others. Furthermore, just because you love your spouse there's no guarantee you'll like your spouse's friends.

Most of us who are married notice that the friends we had before marriage are not the same as those after marriage. Look at your wedding pictures. How many of those people do you still regard as close friends? For most of us, only those who were friends of *both* spouses before marriage remain friends after marriage.

Friendships are more difficult to develop than most people think. And they depend on individual taste. In general, there is nothing wrong with people I don't like, and there is nothing wonderful about people I do like. It seems that I'm programmed for certain people and not for others. Most people find this true.

After I convinced Joan that she needed to choose friends they both liked, she eventually eased out of her relationship with Bev. They have since formed new friendships, and Joan is just as happy with her new friends as she was with Bev. And her new friendships help her deposit love units in Craig's Love Bank.

"You Like Her Too Much"

Another common problem with friendships is the opposite of the last one. You come to like your spouse's friend *too* much. When you find yourself infatuated with a mutual friend, you're headed for deep trouble.

Tom and his wife, Alice, bought a mobile home in a resort community when they retired. They liked the area so much they encouraged their best friends, George and Emma, to buy the home for sale next door to them. It turned out to be a great idea, until George died.

After his death, the three of them remained very good friends. Tom was more than willing to help Emma with repairs, and he often went over just to keep her company. Within a few months he had fallen in love with her. He didn't tell Alice about it, but he did tell Emma. She was also in love with him. Before long he was doing more than keeping her company!

This went on for over a year before Alice caught them. They were both ashamed and begged her forgiveness, but she could not be consoled.

Do you forgive your friend's offenses and continue the relationship? Or do you abandon the relationship forever?

This problem affects married couples of all ages. It is particularly troublesome among retired couples who have been lifelong friends. I know of more than twenty cases where the offending spouse was over seventy years of age. It's remarkable, yet predictable. Why *wouldn't* you fall in love with a lifelong friend?

Tom made his first mistake when he failed to tell Alice he was falling in love with Emma. If he had avoided the Love Buster dishonesty, the problem might have been nipped in the bud. Many affairs in the making can be safely sidetracked with honesty.

Tom had a million excuses why he kept the truth from Alice: He didn't want to hurt her feelings; he knew how important Emma's friendship was to Alice; it was a short-term fling that would end soon, with no one the wiser.

Dishonesty always has its reasons. But it always brings the same result—solutions to marital problems become impossible because information critical to a solution is distorted.

Tom's second mistake was that he developed an annoying activity. His relationship with Emma was good for him but bad for Alice. He gained pleasure at her expense. His "activity," the affair, inflicted unbearable pain on Alice, once it was uncovered. He did not protect her from his own selfish behavior.

When they came to see me for counseling, first I taught Tom the importance of honesty. Over the next few weeks, he told Alice everything. She was terribly upset by his revelations, but she recovered. He promised her he would never lie to her about anything again, even if it might hurt her feelings.

We then designed a plan to break Tom's habit of seeing Emma. I recommended they sell their mobile home and move to another retirement community in another state. Years of experience have taught me that people cannot be trusted with former lovers, and the close proximity to Emma would have been extremely hard on Alice.

The move was difficult, but it prevented him from yielding to the occasional temptation to see Emma, and it kept Alice from worrying about their seeing each other behind her back.

Tom was willing to make the move, even though he still loved Emma. He believed he could be trusted and thought the move was unnecessary, but he agreed, because he wanted to put Alice's mind at ease and had confidence in my recommendation.

They eventually restored romance to their marriage, and while it was a painful process, the positive outcome was something neither of them believed was possible. They had narrowly escaped marital and emotional disaster.

Let Me Emphasize . . .

Many conflicts regarding friends and relatives pit the interests of a spouse against those of the friends and relatives. In our first example, Ellen had to decide whether her parents or her husband were her highest priority. When she picked her parents, she risked the loss of romantic love in her marriage, a poor choice. But when she returned her priority to her husband, their love was restored, and her parents eventually made the adjustment.

I could have related many other examples of parents' influence in marriage. One particularly difficult type of case is where the parents' judgment seems clearly superior to the couple's. But even in those cases, it's wiser in the long run for the couple to make the final decisions for themselves, taking each other's emotional reactions into account. Parental wisdom sometimes fails to take romantic love into account, and unless a couple applies the Policy of Joint Agreement to their comflict, the solution will sacrifice romantic love.

Judy and Bill's case represented another type of marital conflict regarding relatives—in this case, relatives with economic need. Under no circumstances should one spouse's generosity toward relatives be imposed on the other. All gifts and acts of kindness should be mutual decisions, and your relatives should give *both* of you credit.

The remaining three cases in this chapter dealt with friendships. Sue and Jack faced the issue of whether marriage should come between past lovers. It has always seemed reasonable to me for people to be upset when their spouses insist on remaining friends with former lovers. But in our age of "personal freedom at all costs," it's often culturally incorrect to appear sensitive to such friendships. The Policy of Joint Agreement saves the day in these situations. It requires a mutually enthusiastic agreement that I rarely, if ever, find for such friendships.

The solution to Joan and Craig's problem was a little less clear. He simply didn't like her friend Bev. But again, the Policy of Joint Agreement led them to decide to pick friends they both enjoyed.

Many who see the wisdom of Sue dropping her friendship with a former lover can't see the wisdom of Joan sacrificing Bev's friendship. But the answer to both conflicts is the same. Don't engage in any activities without the enthusiastic support of your spouse. Otherwise the relationship becomes a Love Buster. Likewise, even though Tom and Alice had a long mutual friendship with Emma, when Emma came between them, she had to go.

Your spouse is your most important friend and relative. No other should ever come between you.

Think It Through

1. What Love Busters are most likely to create conflicts involving relatives and friends?
2. How does the Policy of Joint Agreement avoid these Love Busters?
3. Think of a conflict you have with your spouse that involves relatives. Is your spouse in agreement with your approach to the problem? Can you think of alternatives that both you and your spouse would enthusiastically support? Make a list of several alternatives you would support and ask your spouse how he or she feels about each of them.
4. Do the same for conflicts you may have that involve friends.
5. Why are commitments to please your relatives or friends of lesser importance than commitments to please your spouse? (Hint: The words *romantic love* are in the answer.)

8

Resolving Conflicts Over Career Choices

Moving is never easy—but it's excruciatingly painful when you don't *want* to move. Jean was in tears all day as she packed.

"Ed, Duluth may be a wonderful city, with wonderful opportunities, but I like it here in Sioux Falls. Please, don't do this to me," she begged.

"I'm sorry," he replied, shaking his head, "but we can't turn back now. I was fortunate to be offered this job, and I can't pass it up."

Jean did move to Duluth with Ed. Then she moved to Des Moines, Kansas City, and finally Minneapolis. Their children had not been in one school for any two-year period and were having trouble adjusting socially. Jean had experienced severe symptoms of anxiety, so she made an appointment with me to help her and her children.

During my first interview with her, she avoided the subject of her marriage and focused on her symptoms. But eventually she mentioned that her anxiety had threatened her marriage. Sometimes it's difficult to know if emotional symptoms cause a bad marriage or vice versa. I tentatively concluded it was probably the marriage that caused the symptoms and asked to see her husband.

Ed loved her dearly, tried to put her first in everything, valued his time with his family, and was intelligent and attractive besides. He seemed to be every woman's best choice for a husband. But in my interview with him, he mentioned that Jean had been cold toward him ever since they moved from Sioux Falls. In further conversations with Jean, she admitted that the move had caused a change in her feelings toward Ed, and she wasn't sure she loved him anymore. They had made love infrequently for over a year.

The more we talked about Sioux Falls, the more visibly depressed Jean became, mentioning on several occasions having no hope of ever going back "home."

I explained to Ed that his wife could take drugs to counteract the effects of all his moving around, or he could move back to Sioux Falls. I predicted that within two to five years she'd probably be back to normal. Even if I was wrong, it was worth a try, because she was becoming so neurotic that her treatment was becoming prohibitively expensive and painful for the whole family.

He was able to get an excellent job in Sioux Falls, and the last I heard, Jean's love had been restored; she was no longer in therapy; and her anxiety symptoms had all but disappeared.

This case illustrates a major point: *You* usually know what you need better than anyone else. Jean knew she would suffer if she moved away from Sioux Falls. And she did suffer. But short of a divorce, there was no way to return.

She experienced a conflict that commonly causes severe emotional symptoms: If she were to choose moving from one strange community to the next, she would suffer; and if she were to choose a divorce, she would suffer. This type of conflict is called an avoidance-avoidance conflict. In other words, it makes no difference what you do, you will experience pain. Conflicts like this tend to make people neurotic. In some cases, it leads to suicide.

Ed's insistence that the family move from one city to another was a selfish demand. If he had formulated his desire to move from Sioux Falls as a thoughtful request, they would not have moved, and none of this pain would have resulted. His mistake cost Jean years of unhappiness and caused his account in her Love Bank to become bankrupt.

When he finally reversed his field and withdrew his selfish demand, two things happened at the same time. First, Jean felt much better back home in Sioux Falls and eventually overcame her emotional disorder; second, the depletion of love units ended, and he began to rebuild his Love Bank account. Jean's romantic love for him was eventually restored.

My wife, Joyce, and I experienced a similar situation, but we handled it differently at the outset. I was offered an attractive career opportunity in Chicago, but Joyce was not at all happy about moving from beautiful Santa Barbara. After discussing alternatives, we came to an agreement: She was willing to go to Chicago on the condition that we would move back if she preferred living in Santa Barbara.

After a year in Chicago, I was offered another opportunity in Minneapolis. Again, we discussed the alternatives, and Joyce agreed to the move as long as a return to Santa Barbara was possible.

During that year, my daughter, Jennifer, was placed in four different schools, and Joyce's father died suddenly and unexpectedly. It was a time of unprecedented emotional upheaval. But through it all she knew I'd be willing to return to Santa Barbara as soon as she said the word.

There were disadvantages to be sure, but there were also advantages living in Minneapolis. Joyce was able to weigh them in her mind and each year chose to remain in the Twin Cities. To this day she has never expressed a bit of resentment toward me regarding the move, because it was a *joint* decision. (As it turned out, she loves the Twin Cities, and she has been very happy living here.)

Is He Ambitious or a Workaholic?

Renee didn't know exactly what she wanted in a husband, but she knew one thing: She didn't want to marry a lazy oaf! So when Jim came along, his tireless ability to work impressed her. He had not only put himself through college but had saved enough to pay cash for his car. It made her feel secure to know he was not the type to pile up debts.

While they were dating, he saw her or at least called her every day. Being with her was a part of his schedule. But after they married, his career took off, and his time with Renee gradually lessened.

"Jim, you're working too hard," she would tell him. "Why don't you relax a little? Let's take a vacation together!"

He would just smile. "I am relaxed! Have you ever seen me on a vacation? I'm a bundle of nerves."

Jim didn't realize—and Renee didn't explain—that the problem was not his nerves but their relationship. They were not with each other often enough to sustain romance. They couldn't possibly meet each other's emotional needs, and Renee had become very lonely.

Renee came to me to express her dissatisfaction with life. She lived in a beautiful home and had wonderful children and all the freedom a mother could ever dream of. But she lacked romance. In fact, she was seriously considering an affair, just to see if it would help.

She had indulged in the Love Buster dishonesty by failing to explain to Jim that she was unhappy with their relationship. She didn't want to appear unappreciative of all the material things he provided. And she didn't dare tell him she was thinking of having an affair. He might leave her, and then where would she be?

Arranging for an appointment with Jim was a Herculean task. He was scheduled for months ahead. So to begin, I adjusted my schedule to fit his. Even then, he canceled at the last minute when a "business emergency" arose.

When I finally did see him, I asked if he felt his schedule was any of Renee's business.

He was puzzled by my question. "Of course it's her business," he responded.

Then I wanted to know if he had ever asked her how she felt about his schedule. He thought he had, but Renee was right there to tell him he hadn't.

Finally, I asked him if Renee's feelings would affect his schedule. If she was unhappy with something he planned, would he change his plans to accommodate her feelings?

By the end of the session, Jim had gotten the message. His work schedule had become his highest priority, and even though he said he was working to make Renee happy, he was actually doing it to make himself happy. He had imposed his work schedule on Renee, and his career fulfillment came at her expense.

They did not spend enough time with each other to meet their most important emotional needs. If Renee had expressed satisfaction with that arrangement, I would have concluded that she was in the withdrawal stage. She would have wanted him gone so she wouldn't suffer from his inattentiveness. But, thankfully, she wasn't satisfied with his absence. She still wanted to be with him.

Over the next few weeks, Jim cooperated with Renee in creating a new schedule. It didn't include the thoughtless activities that peppered his old schedule. Instead, each event on his calendar met with her approval, and his career no longer withdrew love units from her Love Bank.

They fulfilled one of my counseling objectives, which was to set aside fifteen hours each week, to give each other undivided attention (*see* Appendix B). During those hours Jim was able to meet Renee's most important emotional needs, depositing much-needed love units in the process.

In the final analysis, Jim was still a workaholic in the sense that he enjoyed work more than most people do. But when Jim gave Renee's feelings a higher priority than his career, he saved his marriage and possibly his career as well.

Renee's habit of dishonesty was part of their problem. Jim had always been willing to accommodate her feelings, but she needed to express them before he could make an adjustment.

I've counseled others, however, who were not as accommodating as

Jim. They argue that unless they devote all their energy and effort into their careers, their families will become homeless! These people have their priorities backward.

Your career should serve your marriage; your marriage should not serve your career. You and your spouse will most certainly work with each other to help develop each other's careers. But the success of your careers should never be more important to you than the success of your marriage. To put it another way, the success of your career should never be at the expense of your spouse's feelings.

I've spoken to many people who are close to death, and I've *never* encountered someone who has told me he should have spent more time at work. If people have regrets later in life, it's that they should have spent more time with their spouses and children.

Flying Into Clouds of Conflict

Any career that takes you away from your spouse overnight is dangerous to the health of your marriage. The more you're gone, the more dangerous it is.

Without a doubt, I can thank the airline industry for giving me the opportunity to make a living as a marriage counselor. Their employees helped me become an expert on the subject of infidelity, because many of these folks were having affairs in almost every way possible. They also gave me confidence in my methods, since these couples provided such a difficult testing ground, and the methods proved successful even under those conditions.

Sarah absolutely loved her job as a flight attendant. She liked the work itself, earned a good salary, and could travel almost anywhere as an employee benefit. Her husband, Rich, didn't like her job at all. She had applied for it without consulting him, knowing he wouldn't like the idea and thinking she probably wouldn't get it anyway. But when they actually offered it to her, she was delirious with excitement.

When Rich came in the door from work, Sarah flung her arms around his neck. "I got it! I got it!"

He smiled and hugged her back. "Got what?

"I got a job as a flight attendant. Isn't that great? Oh, I'm so happy!"

Rich's smile faded. But Sarah didn't notice. She ran all around their apartment, screaming, "I got it!"

"Hey, wait a minute, Sarah, you didn't tell me you were applying for a new job. Don't you like the one you already have?"

"It was okay, but I never thought I'd be able to work as a flight attendant. It's all right with you, isn't it?"

Rich didn't seem to have a choice. "Well, I guess we can try it for a while to see how it works, but I'm not too crazy about your being away so much."

Six months later, the job was becoming a major issue in their marriage. Rich was not only being left alone for up to three nights at a time, but he was becoming jealous of the pilots and passengers who would ask his wife out to dinner. Sarah would come home to find a beast in her apartment, and by the time he'd settle down, she'd be off on another trip.

When they came for counseling, Sarah was not sure she was in love with Rich anymore, because he had become so abusive. She thought she might be falling in love with someone she met on a flight. A separation might be a good idea, she suggested, so she could decide how she felt about her marriage.

Rich didn't know about any of this and simply wanted me to tell her to quit her job.

The marriage hung together by a thread. Even though she engaged in the Love Buster annoying activities, it would have been foolish to tell her to stop. I would not only have been making a demand, which I don't believe in doing, but she probably wouldn't have shown up for the next appointment.

So I had to begin therapy with Rich. He was guilty of angry outbursts, disrespectful judgments, and selfish demands. While it's true that they were in response to the pain he felt over her job, they had not resolved the problem and had caused Sarah to lose romantic love for him.

I explained that he would need to learn to control his abusive behavior before we could work on her annoying behavior. It was in *his* best interests to control his temper and stop making demands. In return for his commitment to avoid these Love Busters, she agreed not to separate while in counseling.

His success in avoiding angry outbursts was probably the most crucial step toward their recovery. Once she felt he could control his temper, she could explain her feelings to him and even went so far as to tell him that she had been planning to move out, that she might be in love with someone else, and that she didn't love him.

Even then he didn't lose his temper. He simply expressed his desire for reconciliation.

At that point in the counseling process, I had the opportunity to explain to her that she'd been inconsiderate of his feelings when she took her job. She had gained a career advantage at his expense.

Her face turned red. "Well, I suppose you want me to quit my job. That's what you really want, isn't it?"

I explained that she could do anything she wanted. I had no right to demand anything of her, and neither did Rich. But the truth was that her happiness led to his pain.

They began a process of negotiation that followed my Policy of Joint Agreement. After they agreed that neither of them should gain at each other's expense, Renee found another job with the same airline company, one he enthusiastically supported, because it gave her many of the same benefits yet didn't require being away nights.

This happy ending did not take place overnight. Many times I thought the process might end in failure. But the intelligence of the process won out over the foolishness of the alternatives. Renee had lost romantic love, but I kept assuring her that it could be regained if Rich continued his thoughtfulness. His efforts clearly saved the day, and once her feelings toward him improved, she was more willing to be thoughtful herself.

What if God's Calling Is the Issue?

I'll repeat what I said earlier: Your career should serve your marriage; your marriage should not serve your career. Those who use their marriages to serve careers, often lose the marriages. This can even happen to those motivated by a desire to serve God.

When he was nine, Al committed his life to the ministry. At a church service, when the preacher asked for a commitment from those willing to become full-time ministers, he responded and never forgot that decision. In college, he majored in Bible to prepare for the ministry.

Toni was also a Bible major and had thought of becoming a missionary. They took many of the same classes and studied together. They dated, and before long, they were in love.

Before graduation, Toni decided against becoming a missionary, changed her major to social work, and eventually completed that major. Al figured social work would be a great background for a minister's wife and encouraged her in her professional training.

They married immediately after college graduation. He enrolled in seminary, and she found a job as a social worker. After one year of seminary, they both came to grips with the fact that she was not comfortable in the role of a minister's wife.

"Toni, we're in this thing together. You have an important role to play," he explained. When she expressed reluctance to accept that role, he trotted out Bible verses on the subject of a man's authority over his wife.

Toni became furious. "Don't you lecture me. I'll do what I please, and if I don't want to play Mrs. Reverend, I won't."

Then they broke into the biggest fight they'd ever had. When it was over, Toni agreed to support him in his ministry. But she didn't like it at all. It certainly wasn't "enthusiastic agreement."

Al had made disrespectful judgments and selfish demands that would eventually come back to haunt him.

After graduating from seminary, Al took a position in a rural church of fifty members. He was happy with his career, but Toni suffered. She could not fit the role expected of her. There was little privacy in the church parsonage, and she hated living in a fishbowl. She put on a cheerful face when she met parishioners, but when she was home alone, she cried.

Al felt her problems were spiritual and that she had not given herself to God's work. Her "rebellious spirit" was keeping her from enjoying the ministry as much as he enjoyed it. She believed him.

Her depression became so bad that she could no longer hide it from others, and eventually Al felt she should see a psychologist.

It didn't take me long to discover the problem. She explained that she was not cut out for the role of pastor's wife. What's worse, she had come to hate her husband, a feeling she'd never felt toward anyone before. Because she couldn't tolerate the feeling of hatred toward anyone, she was on the brink of suicide. She thought she might be possessed.

Al had imposed his career on Toni, even though he knew she suffered from it. He also demanded that she perform duties to further his ministry, even though they were painful to her.

The solution to their problem started with eliminating the mistakes that created it. I convinced Al that disrespectful judgments were not at all helpful. Pastors are in the habit of making moral judgments from the pulpit and often carry their preaching into their home. Al was no exception, and Toni had become a captive audience. He had to learn to talk to her without any reference to "shoulds" and "oughts."

He also came to understand the destructiveness of his selfish demands. He learned not to try to force her into any particular role in the church, hoping that she would eventually find a comfortable way to help him.

Unfortunately, Toni had developed such an aversion to the entire scene that they both eventually came to the conclusion that he needed to make a career change to accommodate her.

As they discussed alternatives with each other, they settled on a career in counseling as mutually acceptable. Toni was able to find a full-time job as a social worker, which supported his retraining. The work was good for her, and I saw them long enough to see her recover from depression.

He has now completed his retraining, has a job as a psychologist, and last I heard Toni was in love with him again. He works closely with churches and supports ministers in their pastoral counseling.

It's all a matter of priorities. In Al's case, he had to realize that once he was married, *Toni had to be his highest priority*. His marriage could not serve his career. His career had to serve his marriage, even though his career was the Christian ministry.

His choice was not between God and Toni, because he had made his commitments to both his career and his wife before God. The question was, *Which is most important to God?* I firmly believe that his commitment to his wife is most important.

Over the past twenty years, I've counseled well over one hundred pastors and their wives. In many cases, the men made commitments to become ministers of the Gospel long before they'd ever met their wives, and their wives knew the seriousness of their commitment at the time of marriage.

However, in the course of life, the men discovered that they'd married women who, for whatever reason, had failed to adjust to the role of pastor's wife. At that point each had a decision to make: *Does God want me to follow my commitment to Christian ministry and remain a pastor, or do I reevaluate that commitment in light of the needs of my spouse?*

In some cases the men have no choice. Their wives may have already left them, and if they're divorced they may not be able to continue in their ministry. So they choose to adjust to their spouses because they regard their ministry as likely to be lost anyway.

But those who still think they have a choice struggle with the decision. They think God will be disappointed with them if they choose to consider their wives' feelings in making career decisions. I point out to them how silly that sounds. How could God be disappointed with thoughtfulness toward their spouses? He's in *favor* of thoughtfulness, not *opposed* to it!

The solution is found in the Policy of Joint Agreement. When their wives realize their husbands are willing to negotiate new careers with them, they will usually take their husband's love for the ministry into account. The career change often keeps them in the ministry, but provides an emotionally satisfying role for the wife.

I planned my career with my wife in mind. My first career choice was to become a minister, my second was medicine, and my third was law enforcement. Joyce didn't like any of them for various reasons.

By the time we were married three years, we both agreed on the profession I have now, psychology. As an undergraduate, I had not even taken an introductory course in psychology, and I had to begin my graduate school training in psychology at the very beginning.

It would have been pointless to start my career development without her support. After all, my career was to be a joint effort with joint compensation. If at some time she had second thoughts about the way it was turning out, I was prepared to abandon psychology to take up a new profession. Without her support, the career would not serve our mutual purposes in life. Her encouragement has made my choice particularly satisfying and undoubtedly accounts for much of its success.

Joyce's career choices were made with the same consideration for my feelings. I support her career as enthusiastically as she supports mine. I consider her work as a gospel singer and radio host/producer to be an effort we make jointly. I never resent the time she spends pursuing her career interests, because she is willing to accommodate my feelings with her schedule and choice of career activities.

Since we are both ambitious people, our career interests could have wrecked our marriage. But instead our careers have strengthened our marriage, since we consider each other more important than our work.

Let Me Emphasize . . .

This chapter contains illustrations of marriages where thoughtless career decisions were made. The Policy of Joint Agreement had been violated. Career gains were made at the expense of the marriage.

Career choices should not be made unilaterally. Both a husband's and wife's careers should be chosen with each other in mind. Furthermore, if a career *becomes* incompatible with either, the career must be abandoned or modified.

Careers should not only be chosen but also *carried out* with consideration for both husband and wife. In the day-to-day pursuit of a career, each scheduling decision should take the spouse into account. Don't let your career come between you and your spouse.

Think It Through

1. How are selfish demands used to force a career choice of one spouse onto the other? What are some of the excuses people use to justify selfish demands? What is their likely outcome in marriage?
2. How can careers become annoying activities? How do they withdraw love units?
3. How does the Policy of Joint Agreement avoid these Love Busters?
4. Think of a conflict you have with your spouse that involves your career. Is your spouse in agreement with your career and the way you schedule your time at work? Can you think of alternatives that both you and your spouse would enthusiastically support? Ask your spouse how he or she feels about each of them.

9

Resolving Conflicts Over Financial Planning

Frank didn't seem to worry much about his finances. He earned enough to get by, and that was always good enough for him. But he never borrowed money.

After high school, he moved from his home into a mortuary where he worked (while he slept), as night attendant. He earned free meals at his part-time job as waiter and took the bus whenever he needed transportation. Grants paid part of his college expenses, and he managed to complete his education without borrowing a dime.

Beth realized Frank couldn't afford much while he was attending college and admired his financial discipline and resourcefulness. While their dates and his gifts to her were inexpensive, they were thoughtful and reflected his deep love for her.

But after they married and both earned a good income, financial conflicts began to develop. Frank insisted from the beginning that all their income go into a bank account that only he controlled. He was making a selfish demand.

Beth knew he was a good money manager, and he wasn't squandering their income—but he wouldn't tell her how the money was being spent. He engaged in the Love Buster dishonesty.

One day she posed an important question. "Frank, do you think we're ready to raise children?"

"Not yet," he replied. "It'll be a while before we can afford them."

Beth bristled. "We can afford children now! We both earn good incomes, and we've been saving most of it—haven't we?" Suddenly she felt uncomfortable. "By the way, how much have we saved?"

There was a long pause. "We just haven't saved enough. Take my word for it," Frank said.

His selfish demands and dishonesty were beginning to catch up with him. The next day, when Beth was home alone, she started poking around Frank's papers. What she found blew her away. Frank had all their investments in *his* name. Savings accounts, money market accounts, and stocks—all in his name. The most remarkable part of it was that he had managed to save over $25,000 in just two years!

That evening Beth confronted him with her discovery.

"Why are all our savings in your name? And how can you say we can't afford children when we've saved twenty-five thousand dollars?"

Frank was furious. "I handle all the finances, and I do it the way I see fit. Besides, you wouldn't understand it, even if I tried to explain it to you. So stay out of my desk!"

Frank might have been *saving* money, but he was *losing* love units. Beth was terribly offended and ended the conversation.

The very next day she opened her own checking account. When she was paid, she deposited her check into it.

That evening, Frank said casually, "You haven't given me your check. Do you have it yet?"

"Yes, I do," she said flatly, "and you're not getting it!"

This time *she* lost love units in *his* love bank. In fact, for the next year, she lost love units each time she deposited her check into her own account. It seemed fair to her, but it annoyed him.

By the time they saw me for marriage counseling, their complaint was that they'd "grown apart." She had her life, and he had his. Their inability to resolve their financial conflict had implications in many other parts of their lives, and their separate checking accounts had begun the process of separating everything!

Their problems began with Frank's selfish demands and dishonesty. He wanted to control the finances and didn't want her to interfere. With incomplete information, Beth gradually suspected that Frank was cheating her.

Frank's motives were pure: He was saving money for both of them and was not trying to cheat her. But his arrogant approach destroyed her trust in him.

Beth contributed to the problem when she set up her own checking account. Even though Frank had been secretive with her about their finances, she should not have made the same mistake. Instead, she should have cooperated with him regarding her finances and complained bitterly about the way he was treating her.

When Beth explained that her discovery of their savings in Frank's name had upset her, he refused to transfer their investments into joint accounts. He knew his actions had been at her emotional expense but did nothing to protect her feelings. If he had simply added her name to all their investments and thoughtfully requested that she deposit her check into a joint account, the issue might have been settled.

Most of us would consider Beth's defensive reaction reasonable, under the circumstances. But it turned into a good example of how thoughtless defensiveness can be. Her behavior deeply offended Frank, even though he'd done essentially the same thing to her. If she had not deposited her checks in any account until she'd reached an agreement with Frank, it would have been a thoughtful example to him.

The elimination of Love Busters and the application of the Policy of Joint Agreement solved their problem. Frank agreed to disclose his investment strategy to Beth and added her name to all their investments. At first he felt offended that she had not trusted him, but he came to realize she had a *right* to the information he had kept from her—she had a *right* to discuss all financial planning with him. Besides, it was essential in preserving her feelings of love for him.

They both agreed that from that point on all financial decisions would be made together, all investments would be made in both of their names, and they would deposit their paychecks into a *joint* checking account. When it came time to pay the bills and decide how much would go to savings, they would both come to an agreement before any checks were written.

Their cooperation in financial matters encouraged a cooperative spirit in other areas of their marriage as well. As time went on, an increasing number of their habits and activities were changed to take each other's feelings into account. They no longer drifted apart, because they'd learned how to create compatibility.

They went on to have children, and as far as I know, conflicts in financial planning never again threatened their love for each other.

Married to a Spendthrift

For many of us, spending more money than we have seems to be instinctive. We usually know that at least one of our ancestors was financially undisciplined. We probably inherited the trait from him!

Shirley had inherited the trait in its purest form. From early childhood she could not resist buying things she wanted. Her father had tried to help her control her spending, but she'd become so upset whenever she couldn't have something that he'd finally give in and hand her the money she needed.

While Joe dated her, he'd buy her things she wanted as gifts, because he enjoyed seeing her reaction: She seemed to live for her next gift from him. Shirley was an attractive woman, and Joe's generosity brought out the best in her and made her appear even more attractive to him. Within six months, they were head over heels in love with each other.

Since Joe was an executive in a growing company, he earned a good living. It never occurred to him that Shirley's buying habits could cost him more than he earned.

In the first few years of their marriage, he justified many of her purchases as necessary for their new home. But she wasn't satisfied with her initial purchases and had to buy replacement items. The closets in their home were soon so filled with her clothes that she gave away many items to make room for a new wardrobe.

Joe became alarmed. "Shirley, I think it's time we discuss something. You're spending more than we can afford."

She became genuinely concerned. "Oh, Joe, are you having financial problems?"

"*We* are having financial problems! My income is better than ever, but you're spending more than I earn," he complained. "We'll have to start a budget so we can keep our expenses under control."

"That's okay with me," she responded cheerfully. "Just give me an allowance each month, and I'll stick to it!"

Joe worked out a budget for Shirley, but in the first month she *didn't* stick to it. When Joe tried to talk to her about it, she shrugged it off as a bad month and promised to do better the next month. But the next month was no better.

Now Joe became upset. "Shirley, are you trying to ruin me? You're spending money I don't have."

Shirley's voice remained calm. "Take it easy, Joe. You must be upset about something that happened at work. I think you're overreacting."

He couldn't hold his anger in any longer. "Overreacting? My problem is that I haven't reacted soon enough. I've got to put an end to this immediately. I'm taking your name off our checking account and canceling all our credit cards. I'm sorry, but it's the only way I can get your irresponsible spending under control!"

Shirley was visibly hurt by his words. She knew her spending was out of control, but she felt he had no right to treat her like a child. His angry outburst and selfish demand were easily explained by the circumstances, but it hurt her nonetheless.

His anger had the predictable effect. Shirley ignored his demands. The next time Shirley saw something she wanted to buy, she simply withdrew money from their savings account. Within six months, all their savings were gone.

By the time Joe and Shirley came to my office, Joe was threatening divorce. "How can she say she loves me—and steal me blind? I just can't go on like this."

"I admit I have a problem controlling my spending, but I love Joe, and I think he still loves me. He knew I liked to shop before we were married. I'm no different now from how I was then," she said in her defense.

Shirley's excuse that she had a "problem controlling her spending" was nothing more than admitting her selfishness. She knew he would be infuriated when he discovered their savings gone, but she cared more about buying that next item than protecting Joe's feelings.

It's important to realize that Shirley really did love Joe. She simply neglected to protect his feelings, and in the process Joe lost much of his love for Shirley.

In the process of counseling, I was able to convince him that she was not doing all of this out of revenge for some unknown childhood experience. She had developed a very thoughtless habit. But that knowledge didn't restore any love units. Shirley had to overcome the habit if the marriage was to be saved.

Joe was on the right track when he tried to negotiate a solution, but when his initial effort failed to change her habit, he should have continued negotiation, perhaps with the help of a marriage counselor.

Over a period of months, Shirley learned to control her spending habits. We used a procedure similar to the one I described in Chapter 4 ("Annoying Behavior"). Her thoughtless way of buying things for herself was replaced with a thoughtful, mutually acceptable approach. She still did quite a bit of shopping, but the money she spent was well within their budget.

Now that Shirley had learned to take Joe's feelings into account, she wanted to be included in decisions Joe made that affected her. Joe had been accustomed to making decisions for her, and now he faced an adult wife with opinions and feelings that were not always the same as his.

With the gaping hole in his Love Bank repaired, love units that she deposited by meeting his emotional needs quickly restored his feeling of romantic love toward her. It helped give him the desire to include her in his decision making, and eventually they learned to accommodate each other's feelings in adult transactions.

In learning to apply the Policy of Joint Agreement to their financial conflict, they changed the father-daughter relationship that had developed over the years to a mature adult-adult relationship.

What if You're Both Spendthrifts?

Financial problems are at the core of many divorces. It has a lot to do with the way people treat each other when financial disaster looms before them.

Mel and Edith were a happy-go-lucky couple who never missed an opportunity for a good time. Mel had a decent job but didn't earn nearly enough to support their standard of living. Edith worked when she felt like it, which wasn't very often. Most of the time, they got along very well. But whenever they had a conflict over money, sparks would fly.

Mel had a terrible problem with his self-esteem, and once in a while, Edith would remind him that Wilber, a former boyfriend, earned more money than he. To prove to Edith that she had made the right choice, Mel would give her whatever she wanted—whether or not they could afford it. From time to time, he would explain to Edith how seriously indebted they were, but it would invariably start a fight, during which she blamed him for failing to earn more.

A point was finally reached where Mel could no longer pay his bills and, without telling Edith, tried desperately to consolidate them one more time. He believed right up to the end that someone would lend him the necessary money. But one day the sheriff came to his home to serve his wife with a foreclosure notice.

Edith had a few guests over the morning the sheriff arrived. She was embarrassed beyond words. When Mel came home that evening, he received the tongue-lashing of the century. Within a week, she had kicked him out of the house.

"When you have all this straightened out, you can return home. But until then I don't even want to look at you. You disgust me!"

"Listen to me for just one minute," Mel pleaded. "If it weren't for your reckless spending, we wouldn't be in this mess. I've done the best I can to keep us from bankruptcy, and you just keep spending money as if it's water."

"Don't make excuses for your laziness!" she fired back. "If you had an ounce of ambition, we'd have plenty of money. Get yourself in gear or say good-bye."

Mel came to my office to see if I could help him save his marriage.

I arranged for an appointment with Edith and discovered to my surprise that she was terrified at the prospect of trying to support herself. She was willing to take Mel back only because he was able to earn something, and something was better than nothing. Not a great motive to save a marriage, but I'll usually take anything at first.

Neither of them were taking responsibility for their financial woes, yet they were both to blame. In a way, they had conspired with each other to create the appearance of wealth. Their motives were different, but they both knew what they were doing. They just weren't willing to accept the inevitable consequences.

Many of these situations end in divorce because both husband and wife become vicious in an effort to shift blame to the other. They punish each other so effectively that before long one or both of their love bank accounts becomes overdrawn, and the marriage comes to an end.

Whenever Mel tried to discuss finances with Edith, they'd have a fight. They tried to blame each other for their problems and then punish each other. Love units evaporated quickly whenever that happened, so

they didn't discuss money very often. Angry outbursts and disrespectful judgments were the culprits at this stage of the problem. Because
they couldn't control their anger, a considerate resolution never got off
the ground.

The first step toward reconciliation was learning to control their
angry and defensive reactions. I helped them learn not to blame each
other but rather assume their share of the responsibility for their problems. Once anger and defensiveness were gone, they could discuss
problems intelligently and with consideration for each other's feelings.

Mel and Edith did lose their house and had to file for bankruptcy.
But because they both learned to avoid Love Busters, their marriage
survived the ordeal. In a way, the bankruptcy gave their marriage a
new start it couldn't have had without a clean financial slate.

With this new start, they learned to share financial information with
each other and to make decisions together. Before long they were in a
rented home they could afford, and their standard of living kept pace
with their income.

I'm almost certain Mel and Edith will have financial problems again
in the future. Almost all married couples do. But when these problems
develop, they won't use the destructive methods of the past that withdrew love units. Instead, they'll use thoughtful solutions that help
build romantic love.

Deciding Between Two Worthy Causes

Both husband and wife often have legitimate positions, but they may
be poles apart. Helping them decide on a common-ground compromise
sometimes takes the wisdom of Solomon.

The issue that divided Henry and Marcia was how to budget their
income. Henry had a good job, but he was always afraid he'd be laid
off and the family would have nothing to fall back on. Marcia was
more confident of Henry's job security and felt that helping their
children pay for college was more important than savings. Saving part
of each paycheck for unforeseen emergencies was a good idea. But

helping their children through college was also a good idea. Which of the two was the best?

They came to my office in the hope that I would decide the issue for them. The solution to their problem, of course, was not mine. They had to decide for themselves.

To begin, I explained that whatever they decided had to take each other's feelings into account. They must both be enthusiastic about their final decision. They'd never quite thought in those terms, but it didn't take them long to learn the Policy of Joint Agreement.

I had each explain to the other why his or her position was important. Henry told Marcia about his fear of losing his job and having difficulty finding another. Having savings that would carry them for a year would make him feel much more secure, since he felt he could be reemployed within that time. She felt the savings would be a waste, since he was already investing in a retirement plan, and the main purpose of a padded savings account would simply be to provide him with an added sense of comfort.

Then Marcia expressed her concern that without financial assistance their children might miss the opportunity to complete a college education. She considered it the obligation of parents to see their children through college. Since Henry had never attended college, he wasn't as sold on college as a necessary step toward adulthood.

I reminded them that they needed to resolve the conflict with a decision that would take both positions into account. The outcome could not annoy either of them. One solution that would pass that test was to neither save their money nor help their children. (Remember, you have to *do* something annoying to be engaged in an annoying activity. Doing *nothing* may also be annoying but, technically, failure to act doesn't count). They both objected to that solution and immediately set out to come to a compromise.

"How would you feel if. . . ?" took the place of "Stop being so stubborn!" Marcia suggested that she work more and that her salary go to their children's education. When she asked how Henry felt about that idea, he pointed out to her that it would take her time away from him and that, if they gave the kids money for college, he wanted it to come from both of them.

Henry suggested that he wouldn't object to cosigning student loans. If they had the money later on, they would pay off the loans for their children. When she was asked how she felt about that idea, Marcia explained that she didn't want her children to face life with debts, even if there was the possibility that they would be paid later.

Through their discussion of possibilities, they learned not to challenge each other's feelings. Even when they seemed unbelievable or unreasonable, the feelings were accepted as final. For both of them, this created a much greater willingness to cooperate. They became more and more creative in the discussion and finally arrived at a solution they both liked.

When their negotiations ended, they both agreed that the most important outcome of discussion was the love they felt for each other. In fact, it got to a point where both had reversed their original positions: He was willing to sacrifice his savings for the children's education, and she was willing to use the money for his savings. Since I don't approve of sacrifice as a solution (love units should not be sacrificed), they continued until they both reached an enthusiastic agreement.

Their ultimate compromise was a combination of taking some money from savings (but not enough to make Henry uncomfortable), and cosigning a student loan that Marcia did not feel would be burdensome. The compromise did not sacrifice love units, and that was the most important outcome.

Let Me Emphasize . . .

In each case I introduced to you, financial planning came between a husband and wife. What should have been to their mutual advantage ended up to their mutual disadvantage, because they lost love units in the transaction.

When budgets are created to benefit one spouse at the expense of the other or when money is spent by one spouse without considering the feelings of the other, love units are lost. It's that simple. But when financial planning considers the feelings of both spouses, it's a wiser financial plan that also builds romantic love.

In *His Needs, Her Needs,* Chapter 9 is devoted to making realistic budgets and learning how to stick to them. If you need help in budgeting your money, I encourage you to read that chapter.

Think It Through

1. When do the Love Busters angry outbursts and disrespectful judgments usually arise in marital conflicts over financial planning? How about annoying behavior? Selfish demands? Dishonesty?
2. Do you and your spouse have a conflict over financial planning? Is your situation at all similar to any of those examples I used? Describe your conflict as clearly as possible and begin to create alternative solutions that both you and your spouse might support enthusiastically.
3. Explain why some would choose money over love as a higher priority. Is it done intentionally after a romantic disappointment? Is romantic love simply not as important? Do your actions make money seem like a higher priority to you when in fact it is not? How would your spouse rate those priorities for you?

10

Resolving Conflicts Over Children

Greg was a single parent of two teenagers, Allan, thirteen, and Vivian, fifteen. The three had a comfortable life-style, and he tended to spoil his children. Since the death of his wife, eight years earlier, Greg had dated only two women, Bobbi and Janet. He liked them both very much, but Janet enjoyed being with his children, and Bobbi didn't. That single factor caused him to break up with Bobbi and eventually marry Janet.

As soon as they were married, however, conflict developed between Janet and Vivian. Once Janet had moved into their home, Vivian started "borrowing" her clothes without asking. Janet didn't say anything at first, but after her favorite sweater disappeared, she'd had it!

"Vi, have you seen my pink sweater?" she asked.

Vivian didn't miss a beat. "Nope."

"Are you sure?" Janet pressed. "You may have taken it to school and left it there."

"I've never taken any of your sweaters to school! Why would you think I took it?"

"Well, you've taken some of my other clothes, and I thought maybe you'd taken the sweater, too."

"I can't believe this! Look, I haven't taken your sweater. *Okay?*"

There was no way to prove Vivian had worn the sweater, but Janet knew her clothes hadn't sprouted legs. When Greg came home that night, she explained her problem to him. Then he asked Vivian about the sweater. She denied ever wearing it and became angry that they were ganging up on her over something she had nothing to do with.

After that incident, more of Janet's clothes disappeared. One day while Vivian was in school, Janet searched Vivian's room and found almost all her missing clothes. When Greg came home, she told him what she'd found. He confronted Vivian with the evidence. His daughter burst into tears and denied having had any of those clothes in her room. It was her word against Janet's, and she accused Janet of lying. In an effort to calm everyone down, Greg said they'd discuss the matter some other time.

Janet was furious.

Vivian put a lock on her door.

As the months passed, the relationship between Janet and Vivian worsened. When her father was gone, Vivian made uncomplimentary remarks to Janet and openly challenged her right to live there. Greg tried to stay out of the growing conflict. But one day Janet could take no more.

"Greg, it's either me or Vivian. The two of us can't live in this house together."

Greg was stunned. "What do you want me to do? I can't kick out my own daughter. Besides, she'll only be with us for another three or four years. Can't you hold out that much longer?"

"Yes, Greg, I could. But I won't. It's perfectly clear to me that she comes first in this house—and I'm not living in a home run by a spoiled brat!"

Greg lost control with that remark. "I think we have *two* spoiled brats living in this house. But Vivian's only fifteen! What's your excuse?"

Janet moved out.

In my office, Greg and Janet reviewed the disastrous first year of marriage. They both thought they'd made a mistake to have married each other.

But I reminded them that prior to marriage, they were highly compatible and loved each other as much as they had loved anyone. Their loss of love was a direct result of the way they'd handled Vivian: She had come between them. They needed to discover a way to complete the job of raising her without further destroying their love for each other.

In my office, Greg laid his cards on the table. He told Janet he had never punished Vivian for anything. When he knew she had taken Janet's clothes, he didn't know how to respond. So he tried to avoid the issue. He recognized now how much she needed him to help her resolve it. Then he apologized for his failure to be there when she needed him.

I helped Greg and Janet decide how they'd handle the situation where she was being verbally abused and robbed blind by his daughter. Simply telling Vivian to stop wouldn't work.

Throughout their discussions, they made no demands on each other and agreed they would not settle on a plan that annoyed either of them. The discussion itself was hard on Janet, because Greg kept coming up with ideas that favored Vivian. She was hurt by each suggestion. I explained to her that Greg did not intend to hurt her and that the negotiation itself was an opportunity to help him understand her reactions to these alternatives.

I suggested that Janet remain separated from Greg until the solution regarding Vivian's behavior was implemented. For several weeks, they worked out this problem together and eventually agreed on a strategy to overcome it.

Janet admitted that the loss of her sweater was not as painful as the feeling of being abandoned by Greg. He admitted he was in the habit of defending his daughter unconditionally, and it was clearly at Janet's expense. He agreed to consider her feelings first in family decisions, the same way he'd treated his first wife.

This was a significant turning point in their crisis. When Greg agreed that protecting Janet's feelings would be among his highest priorities, the crisis was essentially ended. That was all Janet wanted from him. She knew teenage girls can be hard to handle. But she wanted reassurance that, when Greg married her, he'd put her first in his life.

With Janet gone for several weeks, Vivian started feeling guilty about the whole thing. On her own initiative, she invited Janet back to the home but never did admit stealing the sweater. While she didn't take any more clothes from Janet, she was still rude and insulting once in a while.

The next time she offended Janet—and it was within a week of her homecoming—Greg and Janet discussed the problem with Vivian as if it affected them both. He explained to her that whenever she hurt Janet's feelings, she was hurting him, too. She had to learn that her dad was now a part of Janet; if she loved him, she needed to care for his new wife.

Each time she offended Janet, Vivian could expect to engage in a discussion with Janet and her dad. Within a year, her rude remarks had all but disappeared.

By teaching his children to be considerate of Janet's feelings, Greg implemented a good child-rearing objective, one that helped both children learn to become less self-centered. But something else was far more important: Greg and Janet learned that once they were married, not even his children should come between them.

This example shows how Love Busters can interfere with the solution of a marital problem. Angry outbursts, disrespectful judgments, annoying habits, selfish demands, and dishonesty all contributed to making a wise solution impossible for Greg and Janet to achieve.

Some of the most frustrating and difficult marital problems are found in blended families (where at least one spouse brings children from another marriage into the new marriage). Because couples in blended families are less likely to apply the Policy of Joint Agreement, the rate of divorce in these families is extraordinarily high. But when they apply thoughtfulness, reasonable solutions begin to emerge, and the risk of divorce is eliminated.

From Perfect Lover to Perfect Mother

Wayne had dated many women and was even engaged once, but no one seemed to meet his high standards well enough to make him want to tie the knot—that is, until he met Kris. She was everything he'd always hoped for, and she loved him, too. She was absolutely perfect as far as Wayne was concerned.

Those who knew Kris well were not surprised by the good job she did as Wayne's new wife. She had a history of doing things well. Ever since early childhood, she was able to focus her attention on personal objectives and achieve them with excellence, one by one. When she fell in love with Wayne, she wanted nothing more than to be everything he needed in a wife, and she was able to achieve it.

Kris became the perfect lover, meeting all his known marital needs and some he never knew he had. She was his lover, friend, recreational companion, greatest admirer, and kept herself extraordinarily attractive.

When Rachel, their first child, was born, her focus of attention changed. Now she had a new personal objective: to be the perfect *mother*. At first, Wayne was delighted with the care and attention she gave their daughter. After all, he wanted the very best for Rachel and knew that Kris could provide it.

But after a while it became apparent that Rachel's gain was his loss. Kris couldn't leave Rachel for a moment, and when they were together as a family, Rachel had her mom's undivided attention. Wayne knew that somehow he had to find time alone with Kris.

Walking in the front door one evening, he said, "Hey, hon, let's go to the hockey game tomorrow night. A guy at work has tickets he'll give me."

"No, thanks, not this time," she said pleasantly. "But you go ahead, if you'd like, dear."

"What's gotten into you?" he teased. "You used to *love* the North Stars!"

Kris was not smiling. "We can't just have fun and forget about Rachel. She needs as much attention as we can give her. What we do for her now will affect the rest of her life."

"Now wait a minute! I'm talking about one evening out. Surely her whole life won't be ruined if she spends an evening with your parents."

"I *said* I won't go. That's it!" Kris turned and walked out of the room.

Wayne wondered what had happened to his perfect lover. She must have left one day, and her twin sister, the perfect mother, showed up in her place. He did go to the hockey game with a friend at the office. It started a pattern in which he worked late or went out with friends most evenings.

Even though their marriage had started to show signs of decay, Kris insisted upon having more children. Over the next seven years, they had three more, and she dedicated herself to their care. They loved her dearly, because she not only took responsibility for their training but was cheerful and fun-loving in the way she went about it.

She wished Wayne would take a more active role in raising their children, but when she tried to discuss it with him, he explained that with four children he had to keep his nose to the grindstone to keep up with the bills.

In my last example, Greg had let his daughter from another marriage come between him and Janet. But even when the children are your own, they can easily come between you and your spouse. Kris's effort to give them the best opportunities in life came at Wayne's expense.

People usually enter marriage with the best intentions to be loving and caring partners in life. But when children arrive, a new ideal—to be loving and caring parents—sometimes conflicts with the ideal of partnership. When that happens, the Policy of Joint Agreement becomes particularly important.

Wayne showed up in my office one day to try to gain perspective on his life. He was falling in love with a woman at work but didn't want to start an affair. Marrying Kris, he thought, had been the biggest mistake of his life. He couldn't go on living this way but didn't know how to change things without filing for divorce.

"All she really wanted was children. I don't think she ever really did want a husband," he told me. "I'm not even sure she loved me. How could I have been so stupid?"

I tried to assure him that Kris had loved him and probably still did. She had simply made a choice between two ideals—being a good lover and being a good mother—and chose one at the expense of the other. She had not grasped the consequences of her shift in emphasis. At the end of our conversation, he was willing to let me speak with her about their marriage.

Kris was upset about the marriage, too. She felt he'd abandoned her as soon as their children arrived. When he left her alone so much of the time, it encouraged her to focus on the children even more.

I explained to her that it was in the children's best interest for their parents to be in love. To achieve that objective, their schedules had to take each other's needs and feelings into account. Her schedule took the children's feelings into account, but not Wayne's. He was doing the same thing. His schedule didn't take her feelings into account either.

I recommended a plan designed to flush out all the cobwebs: a vacation for just the two of them.

It seemed like a miracle. During their vacation together the old Kris returned. Wayne couldn't believe it. He became the center of her attention again, and it brought the best out in him.

When they came back, I saw them immediately. Habits are often conditioned by environment, and I knew Kris was likely to revert to old habits upon her arrival home. Sure enough, as soon as she got home with the children, her twin sister, the perfect mother, arrived!

But they were prepared. They had already agreed on a schedule that would allow them to be together without the children fifteen hours each week. As part of the overall agreement, Wayne scheduled an additional fifteen hours for Kris and his children.

At first Wayne didn't think he could find thirty hours to spend alone with Kris and their children. As they discussed his schedule together, he saw he engaged in numerous activities and interests that did not have Kris's enthusiastic support. Since they'd agreed to apply the Policy of Joint Agreement to all their behavior, he abandoned these activities and interests in favor of those he could share with Kris, and in the end everything fell into place.

They'd made the mistake of failing to take each other's feelings into account. Unilaterally, they created habits and activities that annoyed each other terribly. But they couldn't seem to escape from them because they were based on important ideals. It illustrated well how even ideals can help create Love Busters.

Knowing your spouse is uncomfortable with something you're doing should be enough to encourage you to change your behavior, no matter how "ethical" that behavior might seem to you. The Policy of Joint Agreement helps prevent you from using ethics to destroy romantic love.

Three in Bed Is One Too Many

Greg and Patti had a great marriage, and when the kids came along it was still great. But they had one fly in the ointment: Susan, their three-year-old, insisted on sleeping with them at night. At first Greg thought it was cute. But after a while, when Susan became a nightly resident in their bed, he didn't think it was so cute anymore.

"Patti, we've got to do something about Susan sleeping with us," Greg suggested one morning over coffee. "Don't you think we need more privacy?"

"Oh, she'll outgrow it. It's just a phase she's going through," Patti responded.

"Well, it's starting to bother me, and it sure has affected our love life!"

Patti shook her head. "If we tell her she can't sleep with us, she may think we don't love her. We can't do that. Just be patient."

The problem didn't improve for a solid year, and Greg became more and more upset. Before he'd asked Patti to help him solve the problem, she hadn't lost too many love units in his love bank. But after she told him to just put up with it, he started to blame her for the problem—and love units were withdrawn at a rapid rate.

Every once in a while, he would raise the issue with Patti. Her response was always the same: She felt it was wrong to create anxiety in Susan by forcing her to sleep in her own room. Besides, whenever they encouraged her to try it, Susan threw a fit.

They both knew Susan's habit of sleeping with them was an annoyance to Greg. In fact, it also was somewhat annoying to Patti. But when Patti refused to accommodate Greg's feelings by keeping Susan out of the room, love units were withdrawn from Greg's Love Bank.

It never occurred to either of them that Greg's love would be affected by the situation. He only knew his interest in Patti had taken a nose dive. When they came to see me for counseling, he blamed his lack of love on his work, his personality flaws, and possible unconscious negative attitudes toward women. Patti couldn't imagine what his problem was, since she still loved him very much.

An analysis of their marriage identified Susan as the unwitting culprit. In most cases, I encourage a husband and wife to come to a joint agreement without my interference. But in this case, Patti wanted my professional opinion regarding Susan's emotional welfare. I suggested that Susan be taught to sleep in her own bed, not only for the sake of the marriage but also because it was healthier for Susan. I suggested that if this habit had continued, Susan might have grown up emotionally handicapped by an unhealthy dependence.

An even more important consideration was that Patti had given the feelings of her daughter a higher priority than the feelings of her husband. Letting her daughter sleep with them annoyed Greg, yet she did nothing to protect him from that annoyance.

The plan worked. Once Susan was in her own room, Greg reported that his love for Patti was being restored. To me, it was a foregone conclusion that as soon as they removed that burr in the saddle, all the great things they'd learned to do for each other prior to Susan's intrusion would take over, and romantic love would be restored.

When Discipline Becomes a Love Buster

Alex had a short fuse. Everyone in his family and all his friends knew it. But when he fell in love with Christine, he knew his temper would ruin his chances with her, so he learned to control it perfectly in her presence. He also had the sense to know he should never abuse her after marriage. So he vowed to himself—and to her—that he'd never try to punish her verbally or physically. So far, so good.

However, he was raised in a tradition where heavy-handed discipline was considered a parent's duty. As a child, he'd even been beaten on occasion. His parents had explained to him that he was to obey them or expect disastrous consequences. Since no one's perfect, he got the disastrous consequences from time to time.

When their first child arrived, Alex expected the same unwavering obedience that his parents had expected of him, and he disciplined his child the way he had been disciplined. The first time it happened, Christine became very upset and begged him to stop. She encouraged him to consult with the pastor of their church, but the pastor thought Christine should leave the discipline up to her husband. He gave her examples of children who grew up to be criminals because women raised them without a man's discipline.

The temper Alex had learned to control with Christine he released on his children. Whenever he felt irritated about something, he punished the children more severely. They grew up with considerable fear of him. But all the while he was careful never to treat Christine abusively. In fact, he went out of his way to be sure she understood that his punishment of the children was a father's responsibility, something that had to be done.

All his explanations never did change her feelings, however. Every time he punished their children, she suffered. It was as if he was punishing her, and she cried almost every time it happened. Even though he had shown exceptional care for her in other ways, the suffering of their children caused a huge loss of love units from her Love Bank.

Finally, Christine reached the end of her endurance. "Alex, I can't take this anymore," she objected. "I don't care if the children disobey, leave them alone! You're too hard on them."

"We've been through this before. Children will not obey their parents unless they are punished for disobedience. If I stop punishing them, I'll be encouraging them to sin."

"I don't care if they sin. Leave them alone!" she screamed.

Alex looked her right in the eye and said, "Christine, I'm sorry, but you'll have to submit to me as you're commanded to in Scripture."

Christine saw me for counseling the next day, referred by her pastor. Alex grudgingly agreed to meet with me the following week.

My appeal was simple. The punishment of his children was also punishment of his wife. She identified with them and suffered when they suffered. I explained that discipline should be a joint decision between husband and wife, if for no other reason than to preserve their love for each other.

I also pointed out that Christine had an important perspective on child rearing that he should consider. A *joint* perspective would benefit their children greatly. It's amazing how much trouble we can avoid by simply making joint decisions with our spouses. We double our wisdom and take so much more into account when we agree not to proceed unless both spouses are in agreement.

I gave them a simple assignment: There would be no discipline unless both Alex and Christine agreed to it. Alex was not convinced at first that the shift from punishment to a system of rewards that Christine supported would work. But he soon discovered that rewards were far more effective in teaching his children good habits. Constant punishment merely created resentment and rebellion.

Alex had overcome a most annoying habit that withdrew love units. In the course of thoughtful negotiation, he developed a new habit that deposited love units. Christine needed his involvement in their children's training. When he learned to do it in a way that took her feelings into account, he was able to restore romantic love.

If methods of child rearing are imposed by one spouse without enthusiastic joint agreement, they are almost certain to fail. More important, they are Love Busters. (For further reading on this subject, *see* Chapter 11, "Family Commitment," in my book *His Needs, Her Needs*.)

Let Me Emphasize . . .

Children can come between a husband and wife, destroying their love for each other. In most cases, it isn't the children's fault, but rather one or both parents, who assign a higher priority to the care of their children than they do to the care of each other. Only when spouses make each other's feelings their highest priority can children be successfully integrated into a family without the loss of love.

Thoughtfulness in decisions of child rearing is also wise and effective. Children clearly gain when both parents can agree on how they're to be raised. It eliminates confusion from mixed messages and stupid, emotional, and impulsive decisions made by one spouse in the heat of anger.

Think It Through

1. Do you find yourself engaging in any Love Busters when it comes to your child-rearing practices?
2. How could the Policy of Joint Agreement help overcome these habits and replace them with constructive, love-creating habits?
3. Identify a conflict that you and your spouse may have regarding child rearing. Try to formulate the problem clearly and list alternative solutions that may gain your mutual support. If you fail to find a solution, consider asking a professional counselor for help.

11

Resolving Conflicts Over Sex

Alice was a very attractive woman. To be more precise, she was an absolute knockout!

Fred was one of the only men she'd dated who was more interested in her intelligence than her body. In fact, they spent their first date discussing how to help the handicapped, one of her greatest concerns. Since they both majored in social work, they shared many of the same values. For hours they discussed the problems of society, and he consistently expressed compassion for the underprivileged. He also had a profound respect for women and treated Alice with that respect.

Even though she had made love to some of her past boyfriends and usually enjoyed it, Alice had felt guilty and sometimes used. When she explained these feelings to Fred, he suggested they wait until marriage to make love. At first, she thought his suggestion was too impractical—but it got her attention and impressed her! She interpreted his patience as respect for her and a willingness to place her feelings above his selfish desires. He earned hundreds of love units for that "selfless" attitude.

After graduating from college, they were married, and on their wedding night Alice was looking forward to making love, having waited for two years. But Fred felt too tired! Alice was crushed and cried most of the night.

The next morning, however, they made love for the first time. Alice was visibly disappointed. He ejaculated after less than a minute of intercourse.

Alice wanted to try again that afternoon, but again, Fred felt too tired. Of course that evening he was too tired. From the beginning to the end of their two-week honeymoon, they made love only five times, and each time it lasted only a few minutes. Alice must have tried to get him interested fifty times! It was a frustrating start to her marriage, and she lost her temper. In fact, she threatened to get an annulment if he couldn't get his act together.

But Fred did everything else right. He was a great conversationalist; he was affectionate and considerate and made her the center of his life. She couldn't have asked for anything more—except sex!

"What's the matter with you?" she blurted out shortly after they arrived home.

"What do you mean?" he asked.

"Do you realize that when a woman is sexually rejected by her husband it makes her feel unattractive? Maybe I'm not your type!"

"Oh, no, Alice, you're the most beautiful woman I've ever seen."

With that he gave her a big hug and tried to make love to her. He made a real effort to improve his sexual responsiveness, but within three months he found he could no longer have an erection when they tried to have intercourse.

"What does this mean, Fred? You really don't find me attractive, do you? All the time I thought you were treating me with respect, you were simply uninterested! Why did you marry me, if you didn't find me sexually attractive?"

"You are sexually attractive, believe me. I simply have a problem expressing it. I want to make love to you, but my body doesn't cooperate!"

"You're not telling me the truth," she pressed. "You must think I'm a fool! If I were attractive to you, your body would work just fine."

On my first interview I discovered that Fred was more sexually frustrated than Alice. He needed a good sexual relationship. But the pressure she put on him to perform had made him afraid to have sex with her, and it had eroded her account in his Love Bank.

He sat in wonderment, telling me how preposterous his situation was. She was, indeed, very attractive, and most men would consider her the sexual fantasy of all time. But here he was, unable to respond and finding himself becoming unwilling to respond.

In almost all marriages, one spouse is more ignorant of sexuality than the other. Usually it's the woman, but in Fred and Alice's marriage, it was Fred. He had postponed sex until marriage, a commendable goal. But that decision left him sexually inexperienced. Since his sexually experienced wife knew considerably more about it than he, he felt intimidated.

When they first made love, all his worst fears were realized! He completely lost confidence in himself. After their first month of marriage, he had been raked over the coals so many times that he had started to develop a strong aversion to having sex with Alice. From there, it was a short trip to impotence.

Alice ridiculed Fred's sexual performance because she thought he was lazy and needed pushing. Besides, it made her angry, and she felt better after she let him have it!

I commended them both for having the courage to seek professional help for a sexual problem but explained that no marital conflict is resolved through punishment or ridicule. Angry outbursts and disrespectful judgments don't bring solutions closer; they drive them away.

Once Alice realized his sexual problems were not a reflection of her attractiveness to him but rather a reflection of his inexperience, she made a commitment not to ridicule Fred for sexual failure. That crucial first step provided the opportunity for a solution to be implemented.

The assignment I gave them—a common approach to impotence—

let him take sexual initiative. She was to expect no sexual fulfillment for herself until they completed their exercises. He learned to maintain an erection without ejaculation while having intercourse. He was also able to explain to her what she did to make sex unpleasant for him, and she made a few important changes in her method of lovemaking.

When the woman has problems with sexual responsiveness, the solution is essentially the same with reversed roles: The man is to expect no sexual fulfillment, and his wife learns how to become sexually aroused by taking initiative. Her husband follows her instructions, and he learns from her how to make love to her.

Alice had sexual experiences in mind that had to be abandoned when they discussed the effects they had on Fred. She also wanted him to engage in sexual marathons from time to time, which appeared to Fred worse than Chinese water torture. By the time they got it all sorted out, they not only made love several times each week, but they found it mutually fulfilling.

When Alice stopped making disrespectful judgments and selfish demands on Fred, it provided an opportunity for Fred to become sexually proficient. As he became more and more experienced, he not only provided Alice with greater sexual pleasure, but he also enjoyed their lovemaking more than ever before.

An individual's sex drive is directly related to the ease with which he or she enjoys sex: The more one enjoys it, the greater the drive becomes.

Think about that the next time you make love to your spouse. If your spouse enjoys the experience, it will contribute to his or her sex drive. But if you do something to make the sexual experience unpleasant, it will lower your partner's sex drive.

Fred and Alice developed excellent sexual compatibility partly because they learned to avoid Love Busters. But they also found it necessary to receive professional help in developing sexual skills. After you and your spouse have exhausted solutions that you've jointly discussed, you may need to consult a professional sex therapist for solutions you've not yet considered. Many methods have been developed to help couples overcome sexual incompatibility, and you should try each of them until you find one that works for you.

Does Sin Make Sex Painful?

Evelyn was born out of wedlock, and her mother never did marry. In fact, her mother had sex only once in her lifetime, when Evelyn was conceived. That single sexual encounter had been extremely painful, and she felt certain it was God's punishment for her indiscretion.

She told her daughter that God often punishes women by making sex painful and that, if she ever married, she should expect pain while having intercourse.

Evelyn married Doug, a quiet, hardworking farmer. They didn't make love prior to marriage, but on their honeymoon her first sexual experience was as painful as she had ever imagined. In fact it brought her to tears. Doug didn't know what to make of it and figured that whatever it was it would go away. He tried making love to her several times on their honeymoon, and each time she ended up crying.

Remembering her mother's prediction, Evelyn simply expected to experience pain every time she made love. Over the next few weeks, the pain not only remained intense, but the opening to the vagina eventually closed each time they attempted intercourse. It became impossible for Doug to penetrate. Evelyn thought it was God's punishment for her mother's sin, carried on to her. Doug thought it was her way of keeping him from having sex with her.

After the first few weeks of marriage, they attempted intercourse about once a year, but to no avail. On their fifth anniversary, he informed her that he was considering a divorce. That brought them to me for counseling.

They were both incredibly naive about sex. Evelyn had been warned by her mother that God punishes sexual impropriety, so she had never engaged in any sexual experimentation. Doug had learned to masturbate but had no other sexual experiences prior to marriage. He felt that reading books on sex was a form of perversion. Coming to a counselor was clearly an act of desperation for both of them.

I assured them that if they followed my instructions completely, their problems would be over within three months. It actually took less than six weeks.

Evelyn had a condition called vaginismus, in which a muscle spasm closes the opening to the vagina. It's usually caused by tears in muscle tissue somewhere in the reproductive tract or a vaginal infection. But it has nothing to do with sin.

I explained to her that her mother probably had the same condition when she made love her first and only time. Not knowing what to make of it, she passed it off as punishment.

I had Evelyn see a gynecologist first to be certain she was free of infection and had a normal-sized vagina. Sometimes an abnormally small vagina can cause the same symptoms and can be corrected with surgery. The report came back showing that neither problem existed.

Then she and her husband completed a series of exercises designed to desensitize the vaginal opening so that the muscle spasm was eliminated. It's a common procedure known by qualified sex therapists. The exercises were carried out daily (a very important part of the assignment), and within three weeks they were gingerly having intercourse. She was completely cured within six weeks and experienced a climax for the first time in her life.

It opened up a whole new world to Evelyn, and she couldn't understand why Doug didn't want to make love at every opportunity—at least twice a day! Doug had to explain to her that he didn't enjoy making love twice a day, and she'd have to settle for three to four times a week. By their last appointment, they had made a good sexual adjustment to each other.

This case is a good example of how failing to take feelings into account can cause physical problems as well as the loss of love units. When Doug tried to make love to Evelyn knowing she was experiencing pain, he made her physical problem worse. He tried to force his penis into her, and then once inside he used quick strokes that were not only extremely painful but also strengthened the painful reflex.

The solution to the problem of vaginismus was a procedure that simply required a very slow and painless penetration of the vagina, enough stimulation to be felt but not enough to cause pain. Over time the speed of penetration was increased, but slowly enough to be painless. The reflex eventually disappeared entirely.

If Doug had simply insisted on painless penetration when he made love to Evelyn, using plenty of lubrication and going very slowly, he would have followed the correct procedure on his own. Thoughtfulness solves most of our problems in life.

If you ever do something sexually that causes your spouse to experience physical or emotional pain, you may lose more than love units. You may contribute to physical and emotional problems that your spouse may find very difficult to overcome.

Solutions to sexual problems follow the Policy of Joint Agreement. The procedure leading to a resolution of the problem must be mutually agreeable and enjoyable. When you're both happy making love, you're on the way to resolving sexual problems. In a sense, you've already resolved them.

Don't Wait Until It's Almost Too Late

Throughout their long marriage, Grace and Ben had been known for the affection and consideration they showed each other. No one imagined the seriousness of their marital problem—not even Grace.

From their first anniversary on, Ben had expressed his deepest love for his beautiful and charming wife. But on their fiftieth wedding anniversary, an occasion for special appreciation for a happy and fulfilling marriage, he gave her a card that said, ''Thanks for ruining my life!''

Grace thought she was having a nightmare. It was totally unexpected, and she cried for days. Ben felt ashamed and begged her forgiveness. But the cat was out of the bag.

When she had finally gained enough composure to discuss the matter with him, Grace wanted him to explain himself. "Ben, this is the tenth time I've asked you this, and I expect an answer. What did I do that ruined your life?"

"Please believe me," he pleaded. "I don't know what got into me. You haven't done anything. It's all my fault."

"What's all your fault?"

"Oh, it's nothing. Please forgive me for wrecking our anniversary." He insisted, "I'm just an old fool."

"*What is this all about?* I will not let you sleep until you tell me, so you may as well tell me now and get it over with."

"Okay," he agreed, "but remember, it's not your fault! All our married life, I've wanted to share sexual feelings with you. I know you've never experienced a climax with me, and sometimes I feel I've missed out on something that's very important to me. That's all."

"Ben, I don't know how."

"Don't worry about it." He shrugged. "We're too old to do anything about it now anyway."

Throughout their marriage, Grace had not put much effort into sex. At first she didn't think it was all that important. But when it became apparent that Ben enjoyed it, she went through the motions just to make him happy. She always thought that someday she'd learn what it was all about. But she kept putting it off.

It never occurred to her that *her* pleasure was an essential part of sex and that Ben couldn't be sexually fulfilled unless she experienced arousal and climax with him.

But she took a very important step that day. She decided to get help and made her first appointment with me that week.

I suggested she bring her husband with her next time and had them read the book *Women's Orgasm: A Guide to Sexual Satisfaction* (New York: Warner Books, 1975). The book not only showed her how to climax but also how to climax during intercourse, a difficult achievement for most women. They worked together on the exercises daily and had never had so much fun with each other.

She learned how to climax and was happy that Ben had brought the problem to her attention. Her regret and his was that Ben had waited so long to tell her how much it bothered him. If he had told her early in their marriage, she would have done something about the problem. The solution would not only have helped Ben, it would have revealed a very enjoyable experience for her that she'd missed most of her life.

The Love Buster that prevented their sexual fulfillment was dishonesty. Ben failed to communicate his frustration until it was almost too late. Although he used an angry outburst to communicate his problem, the revealed truth was more constructive than the anger was destructive. Grace recovered from the pain quickly because it was so out of character for Ben. In other words, his angry message was not a habit but rather a single act for which he later apologized.

When Grace discovered the problem, she eagerly set out to solve it. To a large extent, her love for Ben made it rather simple to learn to climax. She trusted him completely and felt safe and relaxed in his company. The quality of their relationship clearly made the solution easy. This is generally what you can expect once you've eliminated most Love Busters from your marriage, and Grace and Ben had done just that.

We're all wired right; it's just a matter of learning where the controls are. If you're a woman who isn't sure you've ever experienced a climax or if you climax very seldom, get a copy of the book I mentioned above or some other book explaining how women can experience a climax. If you go through the recommended exercises and still can't quite get it, consider the help of an experienced sex therapist.

An effective sex therapist usually won't mind if your husband is part of each counseling session. It should be up to you. All exercises should be in the privacy of your own home, either by yourself or with your husband. A therapist should never touch you or have you experience any form of sexual arousal in the office. Therapy for most sex-related marital problems is completed within three months and is sometimes covered by health insurance.

If you're at all uncomfortable with one therapist, go to another.

Your gynecologist should be able to recommend several, and you may wish to consult with two or three before you settle on one.

Sex Should Be Shared

Whenever a client tells me her husband is impotent, I'm a little suspicious. While I've treated many men who were truly impotent, more often than not the problem turns out not to be impotence at all, but rather, excessive masturbation.

I once counseled a man who brought himself to ten climaxes each day. By the time his wife wanted to make love, he was sexually exhausted! When he stopped masturbating, he had absolutely no problem at all making love to her.

But that wasn't Jerry's problem. He could do both. If Jane, his wife, ever wanted to make love, he was ready and able. He initiated love-making on a regular basis himself. But every once in a while she would discover evidence that he'd been masturbating. It made her furious—so much so that she made an appointment for marriage counseling.

When Jerry discussed the problem with me, he couldn't understand why she was upset. "Why should she care if I masturbate? We make love whenever she wants, don't we? And I'm an excellent lover besides. What's her problem?"

Jane had explained to him that she wanted all of his sexual feelings to be directed toward her. She felt that his masturbation was like a mistress, and she didn't want to share his sexual feelings with a fantasy.

I explained to him that whenever he masturbated, he was doing something that he enjoyed but that she hated. Her alternative for him wasn't unreasonable either: She was willing to make love to him anytime he wanted.

Then came the real dilemma. He confessed that he enjoyed masturbation more than he enjoyed sex with his wife. He wasn't sure if he could stop.

Masturbation had become such a pleasurable experience for him that sex with his wife was sometimes boring in contrast. He made love to her out of duty and did a good job of it. But he looked forward to masturbating more than anything else. He felt that since no other woman was involved it was okay for him to develop a sexual procedure that brought him so much pleasure.

But he actually *had* another lover: himself! Jane had good reason to feel jealous. Some of the effects of an affair were developing in his marriage: He was robbing his wife of some of the very best feelings he could have toward her, sexual feelings. All those love units that could have been deposited in her account were squandered.

I also mentioned to him that many men I've counseled with sexual perversions—such as making obscene telephone calls and exposing themselves in public—started with an effective program of masturbation. Perversions are usually avoided when a man brings his wife into his sexual experiences and limits his sexual activities to those they mutually enjoy.

I recommended to him that, if at all possible, sexual feelings be reserved for marital lovemaking. He should avoid sexual fantasies if they didn't involve his wife; he should avoid sexual arousal if his wife were not present; and he should most certainly never experience a climax unless it was while making love to his wife.

In this case, my recommendations were followed, and Jerry was able to overcome his habit of masturbating. He knew this Love Buster offended Jane, but he had done it anyway because he enjoyed it. In other words, he gained at her expense. When he decided to protect her feelings, he stopped masturbating. It also may have prevented him from forming an embarrassing and potentially career-threatening sexual perversion. But most important, it helped build romantic love for both of them.

Let Me Emphasize . . .

We've seen in this chapter how sexual behavior can come between a husband and wife. Sex, a tool to help bring a man and a woman together in marriage, can actually drive them apart when it achieves a status higher than the marriage itself or is overlooked and ignored.

Years ago, as I was trying to improve my marriage counseling technique (almost every couple I counseled was getting divorced!), I abandoned emphasis on "communication" and switched to simply improving sex in marriage. I was an instant success! The couples I counseled not only restored their love for each other, but they referred many of their friends to me.

Today, I balance my emphasis across many marital needs but haven't forgotten that, without a good sexual relationship, a marriage is usually in serious trouble. If a marriage counselor succeeds in getting a sexual relationship on track, clients feel that the money they've spent for counseling has been well worth it!

The trick to solving sexual problems is to make certain that sexual desires and behavior do not come between a husband and wife. It's easy to see how in-laws, children, or a career can come between spouses, but sex can also be a very important agent of marital destruction, particularly when it is self-serving and not in the interest of *both* spouses.

One of the most important marital skills is the ability to make love with sexual arousal and climax. All married couples need to develop that skill so they can provide sexual fulfillment for each other. In *His Needs, Her Needs*, I devote Chapter 4 to that subject.

We've come to the end of a section that describes marital conflicts that are relatively easy to solve once Love Busters are overcome. But the next section of the book describes Love Busters that are extremely difficult to overcome. And when they're overcome, they've done so much damage that romantic love is difficult to restore.

It is important to include these Love Busters, because they are pervasive in our society and can lead to unending and almost intolerable pain. Their elimination ranks in importance among the cures of our worst and most destructive diseases.

In this section, I will not emphasize how these Love Busters are overcome. A description of successful methods requires much more space than we have left. Instead, I'll show you how to restore romantic love once these Love Busters have been eliminated. In most cases, they've had such a destructive effect that couples give up hope of being in love with each other. But my experience demonstrates that, even in these cases, romantic love can be restored.

Think It Through

1. Describe how Love Busters can prevent a couple from resolving a sexual conflict. Do any of these habits interfere with solutions to your sexual conflicts?

2. In each case presented in this chapter, how was the Policy of Joint Agreement applied to create a solution? Remember, it's okay to search for alternatives from professional sources. But the final decision must be made enthusiastically by you and your spouse.

3. Do you and your spouse have any sexual conflicts? What are they? What solutions might work to resolve them? Are you willing to seek professional advice if none of your solutions work or meet with mutual agreement?

4. Is you sexual pleasure more important to you than the interests of your spouse? The answer to this question sometimes reveals the nature of a sexual conflict. Only when you regard your spouse's interests as more important than your sexual pleasures will you be likely to experience sexual fulfillment.

Part Three

Recovering From Devastating Love Busters

12

Recovering From the Love Buster
Drug or Alcohol Addiction

Herb and Char were raised in a religious setting, where the use of alcohol was strictly forbidden. The idea that Herb could become an alcoholic seemed preposterous.

It all started in high school. At a party one evening, Herb had his first taste of alcohol. He drank way too much but was able to get home and in bed without his parents knowing he'd been drunk. The same thing happened on a few other occasions, and while his closest school friends knew what was going on, none of them went to his church.

When he married Char, she never knew about his drinking in high school. Since she was dead-set against the use of all alcoholic beverages, he didn't dare drink in her presence.

As an attorney with his own practice, it wasn't too difficult for Herb to figure out ways to slip gin, his favorite drink, into his office. There he would drink enough to satisfy his addiction but not enough to be drunk or to cause failure in the performance of his duties.

He and Char attended church regularly. He even served as a trustee. But none of his friends at church suspected his addiction.

Over a period of years, their marriage suffered. Herb spent little time at home, and when he was there, he had a low tolerance for conflict. Char walked on eggshells and wasn't able to understand what bothered him. She knew he was under constant pressure at work and thought his emotional distance was caused by a preoccupation with his cases.

Since she had never tasted alcohol herself or known anyone who drank, she never knew when he'd been drinking. He'd always been quiet at home, and his silence was a great way to avoid discovery when he had too much to drink.

After a few years, Herb discovered a way to drink at home. He took a bottle of windshield washer fluid, emptied it, and put in a gallon of gin with blue food coloring. He kept the bottle in the closet near his garage.

It worked like a charm. Each time he felt like a drink, he stepped into the closet and took a swig.

Both at work and at home he was falling farther and farther into the pit of addiction. Char found him increasingly distant and unempathetic. He seemed to have lost his personality somewhere along the line. She spent many days in tears, reflecting on the nightmare her marriage had become. Yet she couldn't understand why it was turning out so badly.

One day it all became clear.

Herb's brother, Rob, came over to the house during the morning to borrow a baseball and bat. While he was there, he put what he thought was windshield washer into his car. When he returned the ball and bat that afternoon, he also returned with some real windshield washer fluid to replace what he had taken. Herb came home that night and took a swig of the windshield washer fluid! He swallowed it before he realized it wasn't gin.

Herb went into a blind panic. He thought he was about to die! Char came running, to find him more talkative than he'd been in years. "I drank this windshield cleaner! Quick get me to the hospital!" he shouted.

She was bewildered. "Why'd you do that? Were you trying to kill yourself?"

"No. I thought it was gin. Quick, get me to the hospital."

"You thought it was gin? I don't understand. . . ."

"*Never mind!* Just get me to the hospital, quick!"

At the hospital his stomach was pumped, and he was sent home. But Herb believed God had put him through that ordeal to teach him a lesson. He knew he was an alcoholic, so he admitted himself to a treatment program the next day. Char was overwhelmed.

While he was in treatment, Char asked me to help her sort it all out.

I explained to her how this sort of thing happens and, more important, how it affected their marriage. His unwillingness to face conflict, his emotional distance, his lack of empathy, and his apparent disinterest in her and the family were all symptoms of alcoholism. Some people have those characteristics when they're sober, but for Herb they were out of character.

Alcohol withdrawal was very difficult for him, and following treatment he was often tempted to sneak gin again. So he joined Alcoholics Anonymous and met three times a week for support. At the same time, he joined Char for marriage counseling.

She explained to him that she'd missed intimacy and a sense of closeness in their marriage. He had been distant and difficult to reach because of his addiction. But the addiction itself had created other Love Busters that prevented them from meeting each other's marital needs. The most serious of these was dishonesty. So they spent several weeks catching up on a lifetime of disinformation.

Herb went back to his high school days and explained how he'd fooled everyone, including Char. He went on tell her about his deepest feelings—how important she and their family really were to him now that alcohol was not coming between them. He also admitted how lonely he had felt and that his dishonesty had kept him from being emotionally close to her.

When he learned to overcome dishonesty, everything else fell into place. He spent considerably more time with Char and was able to express his feelings openly. He had nothing to hide. It created emotional bonding that Char had been lacking for years. It also helped him bond to her. Their romantic love was restored.

Marital Therapy Begins When Addiction Ends

In marriage, as in our society as a whole, drug and alcohol addiction has played an incredibly negative role. Besides being physically and emotionally harmful to the person using the addicting substances, drugs and alcohol indirectly harm those whose lives touch the addict. His addiction makes him insensitive to the feelings of those who care for him, and he will stop at nothing to feed it. Many lives have been ruined in trying to rehabilitate an addict.

The addict's highest priority in life is using the addicting substance. Even though he knows his use of drugs or alcohol causes his spouse intolerable pain, he continues his use and is willing to let his spouse suffer.

Addiction is a clear example of a Love Buster. While it falls into the category of annoying behavior, its effect is so extreme we should reclassify it as *painful* behavior. It's not only painful in its own right but it also helps create other painful habits that make the addict a miserable marriage partner.

Addicts commonly engage in painful habits while under the influence. For example, acts of infidelity are characteristic of alcoholics. The fact that he is drunk at the time is no consolation to a grief-stricken woman who finds her husband in bed with another woman.

Women often suffer cruel physical and emotional abuse from their addicted husbands. Even when he is not abusive, he's often disgusting in the way he talks and behaves when he's under the influence.

Children of alcoholics, particularly girls, suffer greatly from the emotional turmoil of their childhood. Mental health clinics throughout America have noticed that a very high percentage of adult clients have alcoholic parents. An Iowa survey once found that about 70 percent of daughters of alcoholic fathers had been sexually molested by their intoxicated fathers.

Wives of alcoholics usually know about their husbands' sexually abusive behavior toward their children and offer themselves as "bait" to prevent their abuse. The pain suffered by these women in the privacy of their bedrooms, during these frightening sexual encounters, is rarely witnessed.

Those of you who were raised by a parent or parents who were addicted can testify to the nightmare that drugs or alcohol brought to your family.

The magnitude of problems caused by drug and alcohol addiction is so great that a marriage counselor is usually incapable of helping a couple while one or both spouses are addicted. The addiction needs to be overcome before marital therapy can begin.

One of the first things I do when couples come to me for marriage counseling is to evaluate them for drug and alcohol addiction. If either is addicted at the time, I refer the addicted spouse to a treatment program. The Love Buster addiction prevents them from overcoming any of the other Love Busters that it creates. The source of the problem needs to be eliminated first.

Marriage counselors usually make a big mistake when they try to treat addiction themselves. Even though I've been trained to treat those with drug and alcohol addiction and have directed as many as ten treatment centers, I do not treat addicts as part of marriage counseling. The treatment of addiction is not at all the same as the treatment of marital problems, and it usually requires specialized facilities and resources that most marriage counselors do not have readily available.

My job as a marriage counselor begins when they have been treated successfully and are sober.

The spouses of addicts are usually so relieved when treatment is successful that they often think their marital troubles are over. While addiction makes it impossible to resolve marital conflicts, sobriety itself doesn't solve them—it simply makes them *solvable*. Once addiction is overcome, a couple is faced with the legions of other Love

Busters that were ignored in the shadow of addiction or that were created by addiction.

The work of a marriage counselor should begin immediately after treatment. Without professional counseling, the Love Busters that remain in the wake of addiction will completely overwhelm the marriage and sometimes encourage the former addict to return to his addiction.

The case of Herb and Char was particularly easy to treat. The only Love Buster to overcome was dishonesty. But in most cases the list of Love Busters that remain in the marriage seems overwhelming.

The remaining cases in this chapter are more characteristic of these more difficult cases. The encouraging part of it is that even when they seem impossible to resolve, the power of the Policy of Joint Agreement has come through to help restore romantic love to these most unlikely marriages.

Addiction Made Them Feel Compatible

Norm and Ruth had grown up together in the same neighborhood and fell in love while still in their early teens. He introduced her to alcohol and cigarettes, and she introduced him to marijuana while they were still in grammar school. In junior high, wherever one came across a new drug, he or she would share it with the other.

They were raised by alcoholic parents and were taught at an early age that drugs and alcohol are what life's all about. Their home lives were wretched, but they didn't understand how their parents' addiction was responsible.

In the eleventh grade, they dropped out of school and found low-paying jobs. They made enough money to support their drug habits. Selling drugs on the side and living with their parents also helped.

After a year of relative irresponsibility, Norm was kicked out of his home and told to support himself. He invited Ruth to move into an apartment with him, to help cover expenses, and for a while life was rosy. That is, until Ruth became pregnant.

They married, and Ruth gave birth to Linda. Those two events wrecked everything. Drugs had always been their highest priority, and they had learned to respect each other's idol. But marriage and Linda interfered with all that.

It started with arguments over who was going to take care of Linda. Neither had learned too much about responsibility, and parenthood came way too fast. Norm's first solution to the problem was to stay away from home. But Ruth chased him all over creation until she found him, so that strategy didn't work.

Then the arguments erupted into fights. Ruth was the first to start swinging, but she was also the first to be thrown across the room. She explained to the doctor that she had fallen on the ice. Norm was sorry he'd lost his temper but warned her not to mess with him again.

She didn't take his advice, and this time she landed in the hospital. There was no way to conceal the abuse she'd suffered, so she did the right thing: She filed a criminal complaint for assault.

Norm was arrested, and the judge convicted him but gave him a suspended sentence on the condition that he received therapy. During therapy his addiction became apparent. His counselor convinced him he needed treatment.

While in treatment, he became sober for the first time since grade school. He woke up to the world around him, saw his life for what it really was, and made an astonishing recovery. Once out of treatment, he never used drugs again, as far as I know, and he still attends Alcoholics Anonymous.

Ruth, however, was still addicted. While at first she felt encouraged by his recovery, before long he wanted her to go into treatment. That wasn't what she had in mind. Norm was becoming a real nuisance.

While he was learning how to be more responsible, she looked less responsible in contrast. Her favorite drinking buddy was sober. Now she had to get drunk alone, and that wasn't nearly as much fun.

One night she left him with Linda, went to a bar, and met someone. By the end of the evening, she had had sex with four different men. It was the first time she'd ever cheated on Norm, and the next morning she was on the verge of suicide.

Her escapade at the bar was enough of a crisis to send Ruth into treatment. The program was as successful for her as it had been for Norm, and they were ready to begin their lives together—sober!

I saw them for the first time three years after her sobriety began. Their marriage was in shambles. Apart from drugs and alcohol, they discovered, they had little in common. Now that they had achieved sobriety, the only thing keeping them together was their love for Linda.

My involvement in the treatment of chemical dependency for a number of years has shown me how fragile marriages are after treatment. Since chemical dependency programs are usually ill-equipped to provide marital therapy, marriages often end in divorce after sobriety is achieved. In fact, some programs I've known encourage divorce, falsely assuming the marriage is somehow the root of addiction.

The first point I made to Norm and Ruth was that marital compatibility is *created*. Because of their addiction, drugs had retarded their ability and motivation to create it in their marriage. During their years of courting and early years of marriage, conflicts were never resolved—they were simply medicated with drugs and alcohol. They hadn't rooted out Love Busters and never bothered to learn to meet each other's marital needs. Drugs seemed to be all they needed.

I explained to them that when they woke up out of their drug-induced stupor, they discovered something that should have been no surprise: They had absolutely no marital skills. Without those skills, the love units, which had been artificially created by drugs, quickly disappeared, and they didn't know how to replace them.

Second, I told them they had come to the right place! I was trained in teaching couples how to *create* compatibility in their marriages. Since they didn't love each other, they would have to commit themselves to my program for three months without any assurance that the love would ever return. At that time, they could decide if they wanted to continue marriage counseling for another three months. I wasn't certain how long it would take them to build a strong marriage, and I explained that it might be years.

We began with a commitment to time (*see* Appendix B). I explained that they needed to set aside fifteen hours each week to work on their assignments with undivided attention and without interruption.

The next step was to apply the Policy of Joint Agreement to every aspect of their lives. Unless they *both* felt good about any one of their habits, they were to try to eliminate it.

They had problems with every Love Buster: angry outbursts, disrespectful judgments, annoying behavior, selfish demands, and dishonesty. Systematically, each time a destructive act would appear, it would become the target of elimination. My job was to keep them both on course and encourage them to continue until the enemy was defeated.

Eventually they could identify and overcome Love Busters without my help. No arguing or defensiveness remained. If one of them felt bad about the other's behavior, it was a Love Buster—it had to be eliminated!

Those with a history of addiction have a particularly difficult time learning to be thoughtful. They learn self-centeredness to perfection as addicts and carry it with them when they've overcome addiction. What looks like thoughtfulness often turns out to be manipulation—they appear to be thoughtful to get their way.

True thoughtfulness accommodates the feelings of others *for their sake*. It is a willingness to *give up* behavior that is offensive to others and create new and appealing behavior. You create romantic love when you do something that is deeply appreciated. It's preserved when you avoid behavior that is deeply resented.

Over time, Norm and Ruth learned to be thoughtful. They not only eliminated the Love Busters in their marriage, they also identified and learned to meet each other's most important emotional needs. By the time marital therapy ended, they were in love with each other, perhaps for the first time.

The Daughters of Alcoholic Fathers

How would you like to fall in love with a person who leaves you for other women, is chronically unemployed, beats you, and molests your children? If your father had those characteristics, you would undoubtedly hate that behavior—but you would probably fail to see it in men you date.

This personality type doesn't do all those horrible things as you're falling in love with him. But you ignore all the warning signs that would scare most women away, because as you were growing up you learned to overlook the less destructive traits of your alcoholic father. It leaves you vulnerable to men who are likely to be just like him.

Adult daughters of alcoholic fathers have asked me from time to time to help them identify men who have the same destructive habits as their dads. Actually, anybody who was not raised in an alcoholic's home could identify them. But the daughters of alcoholic fathers seem to need a little help.

Laura was the daughter of an alcoholic. She'd been divorced five times before she made her first appointment with me, and she was only thirty-seven! The longest any marriage lasted was three years—the shortest was three months, the time it took to get the divorce. Fortunately she had no children.

Laura was in love again, and this time she wanted her marriage to work. She had met her fiancé, Matt, two months earlier. He'd also been divorced several times. He had five children from an assortment of wives and lovers but didn't have custody.

He was living with Laura because he was "temporarily" out of work and had also borrowed about $1,000 from her. At forty-six, he was broke and a recovering alcoholic.

When I asked them why they thought this marriage would work when the others had failed, Laura explained that this time she hoped a counselor would help them correct their past mistakes.

I told Laura I could help them correct past mistakes if they'd commit themselves to a supervised courtship of at least one year. They could not live together during that time, and Matt had to repay the money he borrowed.

Matt was furious.

We all make a living somehow. Some work for their pay, and others don't. Matt was one of those who didn't work. He made his money living with vulnerable women. But this woman was different from some of the others: He was in love with Laura, at least at the moment.

I told them to make another appointment when they were living in separate apartments. I didn't really expect to see them again, but three months later, there they were. Matt had found a job and moved into a rooming house. He had even paid back part of they money he owed Laura.

Apparently my blunt observations regarding Matt made sense to Laura, and she'd kicked him out. But they had enough love for each other to try my courtship plan.

Matt's marriages had failed because he was self-centered and inconsiderate. Matt had learned many of his inconsiderate habits while he was addicted to alcohol but never learned to overcome them after he became sober.

Laura had seen those characteristics in her father, but because she loved him, she overlooked them in the men she dated. While most women are warned by self-centered behavior, she was blinded to those signs. When men said the right words, that's all she heard.

The men Laura married were more concerned with what they'd *get* than with what they had to *give*. Their marital *needs* motivated them to marry, but their inability and unwillingness to *meet* marital needs guaranteed divorce.

The first step I took in helping to create compatibility was to overcome dishonesty. I asked Matt to reveal to Laura any part of his past that could be a threat to her. I explained that good marriages are based on trust, and if he was hiding something that could later hurt her, he should come clean now.

At the risk of losing Laura, Matt admitted he had served time in prison for assaulting one of his former wives and that he had originally been interested in Laura so she'd support him financially. He also mentioned that one of his children would not see him because he had beaten him two years earlier.

He was willing to answer any and all questions she had for him and allowed her to speak to any of his former wives, girlfriends, children, relatives, or friends. I encouraged her to take him up on his offer and gather as much information as she could from the people who knew him at various times in his life.

I explained to them that all his irresponsible behavior, much of it done while he was using drugs, reflected a basic self-centeredness he had not yet overcome! The fact that he'd been sober for two years was only the first step toward preparing for marriage. The destructive behavior of his past was a present threat to Laura.

Matt was encouraged to do a background check on Laura, too. Each man he spoke to told him she was great to be with until they were married, then she turned mean. Even her brother and sisters told him she was incredibly hard to get along with.

I kept reminding them that the best prediction of the future is found in the past. Unless tremendous effort is made, we all tend to make the same mistakes throughout life.

After they had both made progress in overcoming dishonesty, it became apparent that they needed to overcome all the other Love Busters as well.

With the Policy of Joint Agreement as their guide, they completed assignments that helped them gain awareness of these habits and then set out to eliminate them.

Then they were ready to negotiate a fair exchange of care toward each other (*see* Appendix A). First they explained what they needed from each other in marriage and then looked at what they had to offer. It became clear that they needed quite a bit but had little to offer.

I explained that care was not just a feeling; it was also a skill. The only way they could meet each other's needs was to learn the skills that met each other's needs.

The most obvious skill Matt needed was learning to provide consistent financial support. He also needed to learn to share all financial decisions with Laura. He'd been accustomed to putting money he earned into his own pocket. Now he put his paycheck into a joint checking account that required *both* their signatures.

She needed to learn to be less critical and to provide him with admiration. The men who had been in her life had so many serious problems that she didn't believe men *could* be admired. Even though she loved Matt, it took her quite a while to learn to compliment him. They worked on other skills as well and within a year had done a good job preparing for their marriage.

I've always maintained that agreements made *before* marriage are much easier to keep than those made *after* it. Since his employment was a *condition* to their marriage, he kept it. She learned to meet his needs as well, by preagreement. None of her former husbands would have believed the changes she made. Demands were out—admiration was in!

So far, the marriage has worked for Matt and Laura. She married a man who was very much like her father, but he was able to overcome her father's most destructive habits.

Let Me Emphasize . . .

Clearly, drug or alcohol addiction comes between a husband and wife. The addiction itself is a higher priority than marriage, and as a result, the Policy of Joint Agreement is not followed and Love Busters prevail. But even after sobriety is achieved, Love Busters acquired during addiction persist.

In marriages where at least one spouse has been addicted, learning to overcome Love Busters is essential for marital success. But in most cases, even after sobriety, they are not overcome, and these marriages usually end in divorce.

In this chapter, I selected cases where marriages were saved because the couples learned to overcome Love Busters. In the course of counseling, they learned to overcome self-centered and inconsiderate habits. They also learned to develop skills that each of them expected of the other in marriage. The application of the Policy of Joint Agreement helped them overcome the odds and build successful marriages.

Think It Through

1. How does addiction to drugs or alcohol help create Love Busters? How does it prevent their removal?
2. Why is it almost impossible to be addicted to drugs and alcohol when the Policy of Joint Agreement is followed in marriage?
3. Are you or have you ever been addicted to drugs or alcohol? Has the addiction contributed to the creation of Love Busters? If so, are you willing to eliminate these habits so that love can be restored to your marriage?
4. Have you ever been arrested for driving while intoxicated? Has your spouse ever suggested that your use of drugs or alcohol has interfered with your relationship? If you completely eliminated all future use of drugs or alcohol today, would you feel resentful or depressed? If the answer to any of those questions is yes, for the sake of yourself and your spouse, see a qualified chemical dependency specialist for an evaluation. If the results indicate addiction, it means drugs or alcohol is your highest priority and marital conflicts will be impossible for you to resolve until the addiction has been overcome. Follow the advice of the specialist and complete a treatment program that will help you eliminate the barriers to romantic love.

13

Recovering From the Love Buster Infidelity

Cheryl wasn't getting any younger and was starting to worry whether she'd ever find a man who could meet her standards. Then she discovered Nate. He was the most incredibly helpful and thoughtful person she'd ever known. He fixed her car; he fixed her washing machine; he mowed her lawn; and he painted one of her rooms. He did anything she'd ask him to do. What a man!

Within a year, they were married, and two years later they had their first child. Cheryl had no idea what a mess children could make, and she was thrilled to have married a man who'd help her make dinner and clean up the house after he came home from work. Every evening she'd make a list of things for him to do that would keep him busy until bedtime. Weekends were also filled with projects. She was delighted to see so many things accomplished, but she rarely told him how much she appreciated his work. If he ever complained about all the work, she'd become angry. What had started out as thoughtful requests had become selfish demands.

Over a period of time, however, Cheryl found Nate helping the neighbors more with their household projects and helping her less. In fact, he became a legend in their neighborhood because he was such a skilled repairman and always willing to help. The neighbors praised Nate for his helpfulness and Cheryl for her willingness to put off her own projects so that he could help others. Cheryl wasn't exactly thrilled with his being gone from home projects, but since she got some of the credit, she tolerated it.

One day, Norma, a neighbor whose husband had died three years earlier, called Cheryl to ask a favor. "I hate to bother you, but something's wrong with my water heater. I haven't been able to find a repairman to fix it this weekend, and I was wondering if Nate would be willing to look at if for me."

Now that was the right approach! "Oh, certainly," said Cheryl. "I'll send him right over."

Within an hour, Nate had fixed Norma's water heater. But he didn't stop there. He also fixed the garbage disposal unit and her garage door opener. By the time he was ready to leave, she was in tears.

"I can't tell you how much this has meant to me. Since Roger died, I've had one problem after another, with no one to help me. And I've been so lonely. You've made me happier than I've been in years." She gave him a big hug.

Nate was speechless, but he hugged her back. Before he left, he told her that, if she ever needed help, all she'd have to do is give him a call.

The next Saturday she didn't call Cheryl for permission to use Nate. She called him instead, and he was right over. He helped her clean up a pile of leaves that had been rotting in a corner of the front yard for two years.

When he was ready to go, she invited him inside for coffee, and they spent three hours talking to each other. She shared many of the struggles a widow faces, among them, her loneliness and sexual frustration. He shared some of his problems, which included Cheryl's constant demands and lack of appreciation. By the end of the conversation, they were making love.

Slowly but surely, Cheryl's love units had been withdrawn from Nate's Love Bank. Every time she demanded work from him, he felt offended. Once in a while he would tell her how he felt. When he did, she'd remind him that he didn't mind helping all the neighbors, why wouldn't he help his own wife? A compliment would have meant so much to him. But she took his help for granted.

Norma, on the other hand, showered him with praise. She also had something cooked for him whenever he came over and made love to him besides.

While Nate's excuse for visiting Norma was that he helped her with projects, he eventually spent very little of his time working. Instead they talked to each other and made love. When he did repair something, she was always with him, telling him how much she appreciated his effort.

Cheryl didn't suspect a thing at first. When Nate came home, he got right to work on her projects and didn't go to bed until he completed them. Their sexual relationship didn't suffer either.

Over the next six months, however, Nate began to neglect his own home. Cheryl's lists of projects began to gather dust, and Nate visited with Norma several times a week. Norma praised every effort he made on her behalf, and he just loved all the attention he was getting from her. They made love two or three times a week but were very careful so that they wouldn't be discovered. Love units poured into her account in his Love Bank.

Cheryl eventually became suspicious, particularly when their own sexual relationship started to fall apart. Nate claimed to have lost interest in sex. She finally confronted him, but he lied about his relationship with Norma.

Over the next two years, Cheryl tried very hard to determine if Nate was having an affair. She never caught them making love, but she appeared at Norma's house unannounced on several occasions. Nate finally became alarmed with her increasingly suspicious behavior. He told her, if it would make her happy, he simply wouldn't see Norma any longer. She replied that it would certainly help and that apparent concession made her much more relaxed—at least until Norma's neighbor called several weeks later.

Nate and Norma were seen driving into Norma's garage, her neighbor reported. She thought Cheryl should know about it.

Cheryl walked right over and found them together. Now she *knew* Nate was having an affair and insisted that he see a marriage counselor. He agreed to go with her but continued to deny the affair.

My first conversation with Nate was typical. He simply couldn't be pinned down. He told me that his wife was perfect; he was happily married; and he merely had compassion for a widow in the neighborhood. But the evidence was so overwhelming that I knew he was lying to me.

I told Cheryl I wanted to counsel Nate alone for a few weeks before I could begin marriage counseling, and they agreed to that plan. The next time I saw Nate, he told me about his relationship with Norma but made me promise I wouldn't tell Cheryl about it. We discussed the pros and cons of marital reconciliation, and within three weeks Nate decided to save his marriage.

His primary motive for reconciliation was his children—by then they had three. He realized he had a lot to lose in a divorce. Besides, Cheryl was more attractive to him than Norma, and they had more interests in common. He knew he wouldn't marry Norma, even if he divorced.

The first assignment I gave him was to overcome the Love Buster dishonesty. He admitted to Cheryl that she'd been right about his affair but that he'd decided to end his relationship with Norma and rebuild his marriage. Even though she had known it all along, she took the revelation very hard.

Since affairs are incredibly difficult to end, I needed to help them remove his temptation to return to Norma. I recommended they move out of that neighborhood.

He had invested thousands of hours into his home, and it was hard for Nate to even think of selling it. But I felt that the home represented a way of life that had enslaved him, and a new home would give them a fresh start. I also mentioned that I didn't feel he could be trusted living so close to Norma, and Cheryl would be constantly suspicious.

They eventually sold their home and moved about thirty-five miles away, far enough so that he could avoid seeing Norma but close enough to his job so he wouldn't need to find another.

We began marriage counseling with an emphasis on honesty. He never had shared his deepest feelings with Cheryl, and he used work to help him remain superficial. I taught him how to talk to her about his feelings and recommended that, for the next few weeks, he spend all his time at home talking rather than working.

In his conversations with Cheryl, he told her how unhappy he'd been with her lack of appreciation. She explained that she had the greatest admiration for him but had simply neglected to tell him how she felt.

Cheryl's listing of projects for him to complete had become a selfish demand. She had to learn to ask how he felt about doing them, and Nate learned to tell her the truth about his emotions. To her surprise, she discovered that when he came home from work, he wanted her to have dinner ready and the house cleaned. He preferred watching television to completing one of her projects!

But when he did agree to do something for her, she realized it was an act of care on his part, and she learned to compliment him for it.

Instead of spending all his time on projects around the house, Nate used some of it to be alone with Cheryl, where they could meet each other's most important marital needs. They already had countless interests in common and had little difficulty enjoying recreational activities together. Their sexual relationship had never been a problem until Norma came along. By shifting time from home projects to romance, Nate's love for Cheryl was quickly restored.

Cheryl had already been deeply in love with Nate, but the new program made her realize that her household projects not only kept her from meeting his needs but also had kept him from meeting her marital needs. Two years later she told me that her marriage was better than it had ever been and that her resentment toward Nate had disappeared. She lost a repairman but gained a lover!

Infidelity, Like Alcohol, Is Addictive

Infidelity probably tops the list of the most destructive, cruel, and perverse marital habits. In my experience, few habits even come close to causing the rage and disgust experienced by the offended spouse. Yet infidelity is rampant in our society.

The emotional pain suffered by the offended spouse is often worse than physical violence or rape. How can so many people inflict that kind of pain on the ones they promised to cherish?

There's no good excuse for infidelity. If a man's sexual needs are not being met by his wife, finding another sex partner is the cruelest solution. He should solve his problem without inflicting the pain of infidelity on his spouse. If a woman's husband is uncommunicative and lacks the skills of affection, what right does she have to develop a romantic relationship with another man? It's a solution that's clearly and tragically at his expense.

Men are twice as likely to have affairs as women, and they seem to be less willing to end the affair when there's hope for saving their marriage. When a man sees me for marriage counseling, usually to placate his wife, I first counsel him apart from his wife, encouraging him to end the affair. I don't begin marriage counseling until I'm convinced the affair—his addiction—is over.

Infidelity is an addiction to a lover. The highest priority of an unfaithful spouse is being with his lover. He thinks about her constantly and needs to call her for reassurance that she's still available to him. His need to be with her has a higher priority than his wife's feelings. Even when he knows his affair can cause his wife pain, he continues at her expense.

Some counselors, who understand the pain that infidelity creates, suggest that affairs past or present be left undisclosed. I don't agree. I've seen time and time again that truth is the first step to avoiding *future* pain. Truth helps you understand the circumstances that create the pain, enabling you to avoid it in the future.

If you're having an affair or if you've ever had one, don't think you're protecting your spouse by keeping it from him or her. Explain it, even if you think the problems have been resolved. It represents the first step toward protection: giving your spouse information regarding your destructive habits. You may lose some love units at first, but without honesty you'll be unable to explain your feelings completely in the future. How can your spouse ever understand your feelings if there's a part of your life you can never expose?

My companion book, *His Needs, Her Needs,* covers the causes and solutions to infidelity in detail. I encourage you to read it if your marriage suffers from that Love Buster. But in this chapter, we'll study marriages that had already overcome infidelity and still suffered its effects when I saw the couples.

As in the case of drug and alcohol addiction, overcoming infidelity was only the first step toward marital reconciliation. Other Love Busters needed to be overcome, and marital needs had to be fulfilled before romantic love could return.

All He Wanted Was a Friend

Dean's first marriage was great until children arrived. Then he had an affair with his secretary, whom he later married. You'd think that he'd learn something from the failure of his first marriage. Not Dean.

When his second wife had a child, he had an affair with another secretary, divorced his second wife, and came to see me for counseling. He couldn't understand what made his marriages so fragile and his secretaries so appealing!

Upon examination the answer was clear.

His first wife, Sandy, had been a constant companion and devoted friend while they were dating. They'd grown up together and fully expected to be married for life. But he expected her to give him undivided attention, which she willingly did right up to the time she had their first child. Then her attention was turned from him to the child. Two more children made matters worse.

Dean knew he wasn't happy with her shift of interest, but he loved his children and wanted them to have all the attention they needed from their mother. He became a successful businessman and had his own private secretary, Kim. She was paid to give him attention and, in the process, became his closest friend—and eventually his lover.

Sandy never did discover his affair with Kim. During the divorce, he told her that they'd "grown apart," and he no longer loved her. She could do nothing to stop him. But after their divorce and his eventual marriage to Kim, she suspected he might have had an affair.

Kim didn't continue as his secretary after their marriage, a fateful decision. Instead, she wanted to raise children, which Dean encouraged. But after her child arrived, Dean struck up a deep friendship with his new private secretary, Joan. Needless to say, after Kim's second child arrived, Dean was in love with Joan and divorced Kim—who was totally surprised. She didn't suspect Joan, because Dean had always told her she wasn't his type. But after their divorce, she knew he'd lied.

Before he married a third time, he felt it would be helpful to consult a marriage counselor. He'd already seen the pattern, and he wanted Joan to be his third and *last* wife. What could he do to avoid a third divorce?

As with most cases of infidelity, Dean's marital needs had not been met. His wives had shifted their attention from caring for him prior to marriage to caring for their children after marriage. When the change took place, Dean willingly took a backseat to children whom he loved, too. Since he wanted them to have the best care, instead of complaining, he simply had his needs met by someone else.

But to make his plan work, he had to engage in the Love Buster dishonesty. He lied so effectively that neither of his first two wives ever suspected him of infidelity until it was too late.

He thought, *What they don't know won't hurt them.* I explained to him that what they didn't know *did* hurt them. His dishonesty was an inconsiderate act, because it enabled him to please himself at their expense. If he had been honest about his feelings *and* his activities, the affairs would have been almost impossible to engineer.

I asked him to let Joan join the counseling sessions. I wanted him to explain it to her while I listened, to be sure he didn't leave anything out.

He told her that he'd lied to both of his former wives and had already lied to her about a few things. It would be difficult for him to be truthful with her, since he had established the habit of lying to the women in his life.

Over the next few counseling sessions, Dean explained to Joan how he felt toward his wives while having affairs with his secretaries. He cared about them and never thought the affairs would lead to divorce. He even thought they were good for his marriage, since they helped him overcome resentment from his wives' failure to meet his needs.

Romantic love was something Dean never quite understood until then. He didn't realize his feeling of romantic love could be sustained only if his wife were meeting his emotional needs. To allow someone else to meet those needs assured the loss of his love for his wife and the creation of love toward the new woman. He began to understand that love is created and destroyed and that he had quite a bit of control over what direction it took.

His practice of dishonesty made it impossible for his former wives to adjust to his needs. He would tell them he was satisfied with their behavior, when in fact he was not. No wonder they were shocked and dismayed when he left them for someone else. They could not see it coming.

I taught him to express his feelings abut the way Joan treated him and encourage changes in her habits when he felt the relationship was suffering. I also recommended that they continue to spend the same amount of time together after marriage as they did while they were having an affair.

They've been married for about ten years now, and the last I heard, it has been very successful. Joan had no children, and she still plays an active role in his business as his secretary and lover . . . and friend.

They Both Liked Men

Until the AIDS epidemic of recent years, most people had been unaware of how widespread homosexual relationships had become. But counselors knew about it because of the large numbers of people seeking help for problems of homosexual adjustment.

Some of those I've seen were guilt ridden over their same-sex attraction and wanted to be "cured." I've seen priests, pastors, Boy Scout leaders, and others who were repulsed by their sexual orientation and desperately wished to overcome it. Others had no such problems with guilt and simply wanted to improve relationships with same-sex partners.

For those of us with no homosexual leanings whatsoever it's a curious phenomenon. But if surveys are even close to being accurate, about 25 percent of men and women are sexually attracted to both sexes (bisexual), and 10 percent are strongly attracted to the same sex (homosexual). My own surveys find that about 10 percent of men and women have actually engaged in some form of homosexual activity during their late teen and adult years.

Since many homosexual men and women marry the opposite sex, a characteristic problem develops in their marriages: homosexual infidelity. In many ways the causes of infidelity are the same, whether homosexual or heterosexual. But homosexual infidelity has problems of its own. For this reason and because the condition is so widespread, I include this case:

Beth had dated only once before meeting Harry. But on their first date, she was certain he was the one for her. They seemed to have identical interests in art, music, politics, religion—almost everything. What she didn't realize was that they were both sexually attracted to men as well!

Harry was a closet homosexual. He was ashamed of his sexual orientation and wanted to develop a good relationship with a woman, so he'd look "normal." Besides, he was planning to become a minister, and he needed to have a family if he was to be accepted by most churches.

While he was affectionate to Beth during courtship, he made few sexual advances. Beth was opposed to premarital sex anyway, so she never discovered his lack of heterosexual interest.

On their wedding night he had a great deal of trouble becoming sexually aroused, and he was finally successful only after imagining Beth to be a man. The fantasy worked so well that he used it each time he made love to her from that day on. But he didn't tell her about it.

He finished seminary and became a minister. Over the next few years, they had three children. Harry knew he was homosexual but didn't let anyone else know for fear he'd be thrown out of the church.

He might have gone through life with his secret had it not been for Ray, one of his parishioners who was also homosexual. Harry was working with Ray on a cleanup project one Saturday when the subject of homosexuality came up. Ray confessed to Harry that he'd spent his whole life struggling with his problem, and in a moment of abandon, Harry admitted he had the same problem. One thing led to another, and within a month, Harry had sex with Ray.

Harry was in my office the next day, ready to end it all.

"Why did God make me this way? I've asked Him to change my sexual desires, even get rid of them altogether!"

"Apparently God wants *you* to handle the problem," I suggested.

"I've tried, and look what a mess I'm in now."

"But you didn't go about it the right way. You've been incredibly dishonest. Is that the way God wants you to solve problems?"

"If I tell people what happened, I'll lose everything: my job, my marriage, my children, everything." Then he broke down and cried.

I continued counseling him for a few weeks, and finally he was ready to tell his wife what had happened. I knew she'd need counseling herself and saw them both the day after he revealed his indiscretion.

She was torn apart by his revelation. After crying all night and threatening to divorce him, she finally calmed down enough to look at the problem somewhat objectively. But it was several weeks before she was able to sleep well.

I encouraged Harry to tell her everything: his sexual fantasy when they made love, his prayers to God for deliverance, and his attachment to Ray and other men. For the first time in their relationship, he was totally honest with Beth. While it was all overwhelming, he could never have developed intimacy with her until he shared his deepest feelings. But once he'd explained his feelings, they were ready to deal with their problem.

He realized his deception had been very unfair to his wife. He should have told her about his homosexual orientation *before* they married. But now that they were married, he vowed to make every effort to keep her informed of the truth for the remainder of their marriage.

They both understood that Harry had been unfaithful. He had violated his exclusive sexual agreement with Beth, and he recommitted himself to that original agreement.

As a marriage counselor, I've always been impressed by how quickly sex builds love units. Sex is one of the least expensive and most effortless ways to enjoy each other. Why waste it on someone or something else?

Just because Harry had homosexual tendencies didn't mean he couldn't enjoy sex with Beth. I wanted them to have the best sexual relationship that was possible.

To maximize their sexual satisfaction, I gave Harry an assignment: Include Beth in all your sexual experiences. Every sexual fantasy, every sexual act, every sexual climax.

At first, Harry didn't think he could do it, because he'd developed such a bad habit of masturbation, with men as the objects of his fantasies. But he quickly discovered that if he didn't masturbate and tried to make love to his wife whenever he was sexually inclined, he could complete the sexual act without much difficulty. He didn't need a homosexual fantasy to experience feelings of sexual arousal.

Overcoming dishonesty helped Harry feel much closer to Beth. That new sense of intimacy helped him find her more sexually attractive than she'd been in the past. Within a few weeks, Beth was meeting his need for sexual fulfillment.

Harry told Ray that he'd confessed their sexual act to his wife and that he was seeing a counselor to help him restore his marriage. He also told his church board about the incident. Ray left the church, and Harry remains their minister to this day.

Even after learning to focus sexual interest in his wife, Harry is still homosexual in that he finds men more sexually attractive than women. But he's learned to invest his sexual interest and energy in his wife, and she meets his sexual needs.

Beth has a much better marriage now than she ever had before. His practice of dishonesty ruined their chances for true sexual compatibility. But by being honest and recommitting sexual exclusiveness to his wife, Harry found that he could be sexually fulfilled by her after all.

I've discovered, time and time again, that honesty brings the very best out of people, and dishonesty brings out the worst. While honesty doesn't solve marital problems by itself, it's the place to begin.

Let Me Emphasize . . .

Dishonesty is the primary agent of infidelity. Without it, it's extremely difficult to get an affair off the ground. But infidelity itself is another Love Buster. As in the case of drug or alcohol addiction, it's an annoying activity that we'll rename *painful* activity.

Infidelity is an attempt to have marital needs met outside marriage. It's often motivated by the fact that those needs are not being met inside marriage. But whatever the reason, it creates untold pain and sorrow for an entire family.

In this chapter, I do not explain how couples learn to end infidelity. Instead, I selected three cases to illustrate the process of restoring romantic love once infidelity has ended. As long as infidelity is still in process, I don't begin marriage counseling. Infidelity is such a powerful barrier to the resolution of marital conflicts that there is no way to resolve them while it persists.

Think It Through

1. Which Love Buster provides the opportunity for infidelity? Which Love Buster *is* infidelity? What other Love Busters can it create?
2. How does the Policy of Joint Agreement prevent infidelity?
3. Have you ever engaged in infidelity? Have you ever discussed it with anyone? Have they encouraged you to keep it a secret or confess it to your spouse? If you've kept it a secret until now, are you willing to eliminate the Love Buster of dishonesty in your marriage?
4. Have you ever had fantasies about having an affair? Have you ever fallen in love with someone else? Have you ever been infatuated with someone else? Have you ever been tempted to have an affair? If you fail to tell your spouse about these "close calls," you're engaging in dishonesty. Are you willing to restore honesty to your marriage?

14

Recovering From the Love Busters Depression and Anxiety

It was love at first sight. Joy had been invited to a party after work and almost declined because she was so tired. But as soon as she saw Howard, energy seemed to come from nowhere. He was interesting, attractive, and had an incredible sense of humor. By the end of the evening, she knew he was the one.

They dated for about six months. During that time, Joy became acquainted with his family. His parents were divorced, and she was unable to meet his father. But his mother, who was remarried, was very warm and welcomed Joy as if she were already her daughter-in-law. When Howard asked Joy to marry him, it felt as if they had known each other all their lives. She eagerly accepted.

The first few months of marriage were great. Howard had a good job and his salary, when added to Joy's, gave them more money than they could spend. There were no serious disagreements, and they were with each other quite a bit of time, enjoying their mutual interests.

But they hadn't been married a year before all that changed. At first,

Howard seemed preoccupied. Joy had trouble getting his attention, and she'd have to repeat herself. He seemed to lose his sense of humor. Many of the activities that he'd enjoyed he no longer found interesting. He even lost his interest in sex.

Joy couldn't understand what was happening to him. At first, she thought he was getting tired of her and didn't find her as attractive. She tried to compensate by dressing more sensually and putting more romance into their marriage. But the more effort she made, the more he withdrew.

Finally, after work, he would just sit in the living room with the lights off, wanting to be left alone. Weekends were no better. She begged him to tell her what was bothering him, but he would say nothing.

After several weeks of silence, Howard started to bounce back. He began joking with Joy again and regained interest in the activities that they once enjoyed together. Eventually, he was back to his old self again.

Joy wasn't happy, however. She wanted to know what had gotten into him. Even though he was more talkative now, he didn't want to discuss his weeks of self-imposed isolation. So Joy took matters into her own hands and paid a visit to his mother, Grace.

"I've just been through a very strange few months, Grace, and I thought you'd be able to tell me what's going on."

"Oh, I'm sorry to hear that," Grace said, looking concerned. "What would you like to know?"

"Ever since I've known your son, he's been cheerful and friendly. But a few weeks ago he went through something that made him depressed, and he won't tell me about it."

Grace's concern disappeared. "Oh, my! Don't worry about that. Why, Howard's had bouts of depression for years. They last a few weeks, and then he's just fine. His father, Ralph, had the very same thing."

"But what makes him depressed?" Joy persisted. "People don't just get depressed for no reason at all!"

"Howard does, and so did his father."

"Why didn't he tell me about this before we were married?" Joy objected.

Grace shrugged. "He's probably ashamed of it. But he shouldn't be—that's just the way he is."

As they continued their conversation, Joy discovered that Grace's husband had suffered a particularly long period of depression, during which Grace had an affair. When her husband discovered it, he divorced her. Grace felt embarrassed to admit it to Joy but felt she should know now that she was part of the family.

Joy sat Howard down that evening and told him what she'd learned from his mother. Howard was furious. He didn't think his mother had any right meddling in their marriage. He felt she'd already ruined his father's life, and now she was trying to ruin his. The conversation went nowhere.

For the next three years, Howard continued to suffer periods of depression. He'd be cheerful and relatively carefree for several months; then there'd be weeks or even months of unhappiness.

Joy had the sense to know they couldn't have children under those conditions and that a normal married life was hopeless. So one day she moved out and filed for divorce.

They saw me for counseling a week later.

It didn't take me long to conclude that Howard had a serious case of recurrent depression that he probably inherited from his father. I've seen many clients who experience this cycle from a normal state to a depressed state and back to a normal state of mind. Same cycle from depression to euphoria and back to depression.

Depression is the feeling of hopelessness: nothing to look forward to; no reason to go on; things will never get better, only worse; my best years are behind me, my worst years are ahead.

When depression controls you, you're convinced that planning is pointless, because no plan will ever work for you anyway. And even if you have a plan, trying hard to achieve it is foolish, because you'll fail regardless of your effort. In other words, depression *makes* you fail because it overrides the intelligence that *knows how* you can succeed.

In a private session with Howard, I explained that his emotional disorder had interfered with his ability to have a normal marriage. He could not expect to fulfill his wife's marital needs as long as his condition persisted. However, if he was willing to overcome this emotional disorder, he would straighten out a lifelong personal problem and give his marriage a second chance.

Howard loved Joy very much, and she had made it clear that unless things changed she couldn't remain married to him. So he agreed to do whatever it would take to get her back.

In consultation with a psychiatrist, Howard began taking a drug that helps break the cycles of depression. Within two weeks, he had adjusted to the medicine, and I spent several more weeks helping him understand what came over him when he'd become depressed. I encouraged him to consider antidepressants the way a diabetic considered insulin: a drug necessary to compensate for a biological imbalance.

I've helped many people overcome depression without the use of drugs by straightening out a bad relationship or by improving their employment conditions. But when there's evidence of a cyclical depression that doesn't seem related to any event in life, antidepressant drugs are usually the answer.

As soon as I was convinced that his cycles of depression were under control, I was ready to work on his marriage.

Howard's recurrent depression had encouraged him to practice the Love Buster dishonesty from the first day he met Joy. As with many who suffer emotional disorders, he was ashamed of his lack of emotional control and tried to keep it from her. We spent the first few weeks of counseling clearing up many of Joy's misunderstandings that grew from his dishonesty.

He learned to follow all parts of the Rule of Honesty. First, he learned to share his emotional reactions, even if he thought they were irrational. Then he told Joy about the years that he'd struggled with depression and the devastating effect it had on his self-esteem. He told her how his cycles of depression ruined his ability to follow through on healthy planning and what his real plans for life were. Little by little, he shared with her feelings he'd never shared with anyone before.

I explained to Joy that, whenever he started to feel depressed, his attitudes changed so dramatically that he knew they were irrational. That's why he'd never explain them to her, even after the depression was over. Now he agreed to tell her how he felt, even if he knew it sounded strange.

He had been too proud to seek professional help for his depression, and his pride left Joy unprotected. But as soon as he was treated with antidepressant drugs, his mood cycles moderated to such an extent that Joy hardly noticed them. He put an end to the erosion of love units that took place during each period of depression.

To protect herself from the pain of his behavior, Joy had entered the emotional stage of Withdrawal. But after he overcame depression and dishonesty, Joy could lower her defenses. Before long, she was back to the Intimacy stage, where love units were being deposited by Howard in record numbers. Romantic love was restored.

At first Howard was not completely convinced he needed an antidepressant drug, so every once in a while he'd stop taking it. But as soon as his depression returned, he realized he wasn't cured and returned to the medication. He finally resigned himself to the idea that he'd probably be taking an antidepressant the rest of his life.

Joy and Howard are now the proud parents of three children, and their marriage is in great shape. While Howard's emotional disorder is probably inherited, and at least one of his children may someday suffer some of the same symptoms, Howard and Joy are in a good position to explain to a child how to compensate and live a happy, productive life. They are outstanding examples to their children of how to overcome an emotional disorder and get on with the adventures of life.

Depression is the most common emotional disorder. If you feel that either you or your spouse suffers from this condition, get professional help.

Since most depression is brief, and often cyclical, it's sometimes difficult to know if a therapist helped you end the depression or if it would have ended without help. If you experience an end to the *cycles* of depression, you can judge the therapy successful. If your depression recurs, the treatment has probably not been successful, and I would advise you to look for another, more effective, therapist.

When personal loss or setbacks in your life cause depression, it's called *situational* depression. We all experience this at one time or another. But if you find the feelings are deep, and you cannot snap out of it, find help to control the emotional damage. There's no point to needless suffering or needless withdrawal of love units.

The Love Buster Emotional Disorders Creates Love Busters

Someone who comes to me for emotional help usually suffers from one of two emotional disorders: depression or anxiety. Of course, many suffer from both.

Both are normal emotions. We all feel them once in a while. But when they begin to take over our lives, they become *emotional disorders*, conditions that psychologists and other mental health specialists are trained to help people overcome.

Emotional disorders are unpleasant for both those who have them and for their spouses. Can you imagine what it would be like living with someone who feels depressed or anxious most of the time? You may know exactly what it feels like, if your spouse suffers from these disorders.

Uncontrolled emotions of one or both spouses often cause marital incompatibility that leads to marital conflict. The couple's emotions come between them. When emotions, rather than intelligence, guide their behavior, they become unable to solve the simplest marital conflicts.

Before I begin marriage counseling, I give every couple an assessment to see if either spouse has out-of-control emotions. If so, I usually treat them individually until control is achieved; then I begin marriage counseling. When I work with a couple's intelligence, my job is rewarding. But when I can only work with emotion, marriage counseling wastes my time and theirs.

There are innumerable causes for emotional disorders. Sometimes they're inherited; sometimes they're caused by a rotten childhood; sometimes they're caused by a frustrating job or financial pressures or an unfulfilling marriage. Whatever the reasons, they almost always have a negative effect on marriage.

Those who experience emotional disorders usually cannot prevent themselves from behaving in a destructive way. They are often dishonest about their inner emotions for fear others won't accept them. They frequently keep their feelings to themselves, because they don't want to burden others or they don't want people to think they're defective. The things they do to try to keep their emotions under control are often hidden from the world, and they tend to be lonely and isolated, even when married.

Those with a depressive or anxiety disorder engage in countless annoying habits in an effort to reduce their emotional symptoms. For example, depression often keeps people from going to work, maintaining physical hygiene, or picking up after themselves. One depressed man I counseled had not washed himself for three months!

Those with emotional disorders almost always make selfish demands. Since emotions guide their planning, their requests don't often make any sense, and when their requests fail, demands quickly take over. They often feel so bad and their intelligence is so overcome by emotions that they can only communicate by demands.

Their condition is like someone who is dying of thirst, and someone with water won't give them any. A demand seems reasonable to them in that situation. But those without the emotional disorder see the demand for what it is—an irrational and self-defeating act.

Emotional disorders can be overcome. First you must recognize that an emotion leads you astray and that you want your intelligence to be in control once again. When you take that step, there are many effective methods available that can help, and it's simply a matter of getting help from a qualified psychologist or other mental health specialist.

Emotionally disturbed clients often try to convince me and their spouses that if their marriages were fulfilling they'd regain emotional control. But I regard that excuse as a smoke screen. It's like the alcoholic telling his wife he'll stop drinking as soon as she's perfect. Just as the alcoholic has the responsibility to gain sobriety, an emotionally disturbed spouse is responsible to gain emotional control. Those who suffer from depression or anxiety must take personal responsibility and avoid blaming others for their condition.

Marriage is a two-way street, and until *each* spouse can treat the other thoughtfully, a marriage can't work. If an emotionally disturbed spouse is temporarily unable to hold up his end of the bargain, he should have professional help to overcome the disorder to regain his thoughtfulness.

I've witnessed hundreds of people with emotional disorders who've gained lifelong control over them and restored love to their marriages.

Overcoming Anxiety

Valerie grew up in a family that guarded emotions—especially fear. Whenever she was afraid of something, her mother encouraged her to avoid it until she felt better. As a result, she missed quite a bit of school. Her mother helped with her studies, so she always had good grades. But she missed out on a lot of life that her parents couldn't make up for as easily.

Chris, a neighbor, grew up with her and became her only boyfriend. She invited him over to talk and watch television. Eventually, they became quite attached to each other. She was attractive and could have dated almost any of the guys at school, but Chris was the only one with whom she felt comfortable.

Chris worked as a carpenter's apprentice after high school and rented an apartment. But Val went on to college and continued to live at home.

By the time Val graduated, Chris had a good job in construction and had already bought his first home. They married shortly after her graduation.

It would have been relatively easy for Val to find a job, but Chris encouraged her to do whatever would make her happy. So she stayed home and did housework. Val was a terrific homemaker. Meals were imaginative, the home was spotless, and Chris's clothes were always clean and ironed. They had a great relationship at home, sexually and every other way.

They had hoped to raise children right after marriage. However, Val was afraid to stop taking her birth control pills, so five years later they were still without children.

And there was another problem: Val *never* left the house—not even to visit her own parents or pick up the mail or water the garden. Chris knew she had always been fearful, but he thought she'd grow out of it after their marriage. Now her anxiety was getting worse instead of better. She had developed a serious anxiety disorder that caused her to be afraid of literally everything outside the house.

One day he decided he'd have to help her turn the corner. "Val," he said casually, "let's go outside for a walk."

Her face froze. "Not today. You know how I feel when I walk outside."

"But you can't live inside a house all your life," he tried to reason. "Besides, I want to be able to go places with you. *I* don't want to live inside a house all my life."

"Well, maybe we'll try it tomorrow. I'm getting sick just thinking about it right now."

"You've become housebound," he pressed. "You haven't left the house for three years. Do you realize that?"

"Yes, I realize that," she said desperately. "What do you want me to do about it? Walk out the door and go shopping? I just can't—and you know why."

He blinked. "No, I don't know why. Tell me."

"Because I'm *afraid*, that's why."

"But you and I can never go anywhere together. I'm stuck in this house with you!"

Val burst into tears, and that ended their conversation.

That week Chris went to his doctor for advice, and his doctor referred him to me. As Chris explained his problem, I could see he'd suffered from the effects of Val's anxiety. He'd been very upset about it but had tried his best to keep his feelings from her, since she felt so anxious already. Over their five years of marriage, he had become increasingly dissatisfied and now considered divorce.

I explained to him that her emotional disorder could be overcome. But if it were left untreated, she'd probably be an emotional invalid the rest of her life. It not only ruined their marriage, but it ruined her chances for a normal, productive life.

The first step toward her recovery was for him to tell her exactly how he felt. It wasn't in *her* best interests for him to encourage her behavior, and his dishonesty prevented a solution.

After our conversation, Chris told Val he could no longer tolerate her fears of the outside world, and unless she learned to overcome them, their marriage was in serious jeopardy. She didn't take the news well, but he realized the next move had to be hers.

Later that week, Chris brought Val to my office for her first appointment. It was the first time in three years that she'd been out of her house for more than a few minutes, and she was trembling with fear. She knew her predisposition toward anxiety had gotten the best of her and that unless she did something soon she would not only lose her husband but all her opportunities in life.

With the aid of a psychiatrist, we combined a nonaddicting medicine that helped relieve her anxiety with a program of systematic desensitization. Over a period of three months, she learned to spend more and more time outside her home, until she was gone for twelve hours at a time. All with no panic attacks.

Val made a sensational recovery. She proved to herself and Chris that her emotional disorder was created, in part, by catering to her anxiety. Her parents had done her no favors by letting her stay home when she feared school, and her husband had helped keep the weakness alive. Within six months she had a part-time job, to make certain she'd never become housebound again.

Once free from the restrictions of her home, Val was able to more freely engage in recreational and social activities that redeposited love units into Chris's Love Bank. Needless to say, their marriage and his romantic love for her rebounded.

Having worked with so many emotionally disturbed people, I'm fully convinced that we do them no favors by pretending their weakness does not affect us. It may be rude to tell strangers how they make us feel, but if we're in an intimate relationship with someone, we *must* communicate our feelings, *good and bad*. Otherwise the relationship will be superficial at best and areas of incompatibility will remain.

Chris made his biggest mistake by being dishonest. He didn't tell Val how he felt about her disability until it was almost too late. Even if he thought nothing could have been done about it, he should have told her how it affected him. None of us know what's possible in life until we try. And honesty clarifies problems so that we're more likely to find solutions.

By harboring a known emotional disorder, Val failed to protect her husband from the bizarre behavior it created. She was also unable to meet some of his marital needs because of the roadblocks her fears put in the way. Most recreational activities were impossible, and normal social relationships became a thing of the past.

However, once she decided to meet the problem head-on, she found it was a paper dragon. She could overcome her fear after all, and within a year she was off all medication, living a relatively normal life and happily married besides.

Let Me Emphasize . . .

When someone suffers from an emotional disorder, Love Busters are usually unavoidable. The emotional disorder must be resolved *before* one spouse can avoid being the source of pain for the other.

But after an emotional disorder is overcome, its effect on marriage often remains. All the love units lost from Love Busters leave the marriage bankrupt. The love that once made the marriage work no longer exists, and the couple often must re-create it.

Therapy is effective for most emotional disorders. If you or your spouse suffer from depression or anxiety, you are needlessly ruining romantic love in your marriage. Get the help you need to overcome the disorder and then begin the process of replacing love units you've been withdrawing.

Think It Through

1. What type of Love Busters are emotional disorders? What Love Busters do emotional disorders create?
2. How can the Policy of Joint Agreement be applied when one or both spouses have an emotional disorder? (Hint: An emotional disorder tends to severely limit reasonable solutions to a problem.)
3. Do you have an emotional disorder? Have you discussed with your spouse its effect on your attitudes and behavior? Are you willing to overcome the disorder?
4. Do you ever find yourself so overcome with anxiety or depression that you momentarily lose emotional control? Has your spouse ever been the unintentional victim of one of your emotional episodes? Do you find your attitudes are so inconsistent that you can agree to something one day and disagree the next? If you answered yes to any of these, obtain a mental health evaluation from a qualified therapist. If results indicate an emotional disorder, it means your emotions dominate your intelligence when you try to resolve marital conflicts. Find a therapist who will help you restore intelligence and love to your marriage.

15

Conclusion

Romantic Love Is Yours for the Taking

Those of us in the business of restoring marriages are continually aware of the bliss of a good marriage and the nightmare of a bad one. We're also aware that nightmare marriages usually start blissfully. The chance of any one blissful marriage becoming a nightmare and ending in divorce is over 50 percent—a staggering statistic.

But that's not all. Many marriages that *don't* end in divorce also turn out to be nightmares. Often couples stay together for financial or religious reasons; some of the most violent and tragic marriages fall into this category.

The difference between bliss and nightmares in marriage is romantic love—bliss has it, and nightmares don't. The unfortunate state of marriage today is a reflection of how couples have failed to preserve romantic love for each other. But it's not that difficult to preserve.

The remarkable truth is that people can preserve romantic love if they would simply consider each other's feelings. Thoughtlessness that has crept into our culture and into our behavior has a devastating effect on marriage and romantic love.

Thoughtfulness is the key to sustaining romantic love. It means *never gaining any objective or pleasure at the expense of your spouse's feelings.*

A couple can find literally hundreds of ways to be thoughtless, but they all have the same effect: They withdraw love units from the Love Bank and ruin romantic love. I call them destructive marital habits or Love Busters. To be more precise, I used this definition:

> **A destructive marital habit, or Love Buster, is repeated behavior of a spouse that causes the other to be unhappy (withdraw love units).**

I've given special attention to five kinds of Love Busters:

1. *Angry outbursts* destroy romantic love because they are motivated by a desire to punish the person who made you unhappy: your spouse. You withdraw love units each time you lose your temper.
2. *Disrespectful judgments* occur whenever one spouse tries to impose his or her system of values and beliefs on the other. The one making disrespectful judgments feels he is teaching valuable lessons that will ultimately benefit his spouse. But the spouse on the receiving end generally regards such effort as arrogant and rude.
3. *Annoying behavior* is usually when one person seeks to win at the emotional expense of the other.
4. In making *selfish demands,* the demanding spouse imposes a punishment if the demand is resisted. Romantic love is sacrificed each time a demand is made. Thoughtful requests can achieve the outcome of selfish demands without sacrificing romantic love.
5. *Dishonesty,* even if it's not discovered, prevents couples from solving marital conflicts. Solutions go unnoticed in a fog of disinformation.

Honesty is essential in solving marital problems, although it can withdraw love units. But failure to reveal painful mistakes is an even greater threat to romantic love. So I have modified the definition of Love Busters to include this exception:

> **A destructive marital habit, or Love Buster, is repeated behavior of a spouse that causes the other to be unhappy (withdraw love units). Honesty is not a Love Buster because the only alternative, dishonesty, is even more destructive.**

I introduced a rule that helps avoid Love Busters and also improves marital problem solving. I call it the Policy of Joint Agreement: *Never do anything without the enthusiastic agreement of you spouse.* It's a rule that tends to guarantee mutual thoughtfulness.

Three Love Busters not only destroy romantic love but also create other Love Busters. Their effect on romantic love is devastating because even after they're overcome, the Love Busters they create remain in marriage to continue destroying love. These particularly dangerous Love Busters are (1) drug or alcohol addiction, (2) infidelity, and (3) emotional disorders.

But each of these dangerous Love Busters can be eliminated through personal, not marital, counseling. Then after it is overcome, the other Love Busters it created can be swept away through marriage counseling.

Making Romantic Love With Your Spouse Your Highest Priority

If you've ever been to a seminar on achievement and motivation, the speaker probably impressed you with the importance of setting priorities. Such speakers often use the accumulation of money as an example. If becoming a millionaire is a high priority, you can become a millionaire!

For most people, the principle works. I've seen high school drop-outs become multimillionaires by making the accumulation of wealth a high priority.

What these seminar leaders don't usually say, however, is that it's dangerous to make these objectives your *highest* priority. Unless your highest priority is romantic love with your spouse, you won't have a successful marriage. Without a successful marriage, none of these other objectives will be valuable to you in the long run.

Which would you rather have, a successful marriage or a million dollars? How about a successful marriage or happy children? Admiring parents? A successful career? Fulfilling sex? Alcohol? Whatever it is, if it's more important than your marriage, you probably won't have a successful marriage.

You probably noticed that I didn't ask you to make marriage your highest priority. Thats because it's too vague. I want you to get down to specifics. If romantic love with your spouse is your highest priority, and you succeed in achieving it, your marriage *will* be successful. The only way you'll be able to achieve romantic love is to put the feelings of your spouse first in your life. You'll build romantic love by meeting your spouse's most important emotional needs, and you'll preserve the love you build by eliminating Love Busters.

If you want to have happy children or admiring parents or a successful career or a million dollars, they have to be *secondary* objectives. You can't have them *at the expense of your spouse's feelings*. A strong marriage often builds a foundation for the achievement of all these other objectives in life. But these other things don't build a foundation for romantic love or marriage.

Building Romantic Love

As I mentioned earlier, this book is mostly about love busters, habits that destroy romantic love. My purpose was to encourage you to eliminate them so you don't lose one of life's greatest treasures.

But there's also a companion subject, love builders, habits that build romantic love. My book *His Needs, Her Needs* is devoted almost entirely to it, so I have not repeated many of those ideas here.

For those who will not read *His Needs, Her Needs* or would like a brief summary of how to build romantic love, I've added appendices to briefly describe the two most important love builders, care (Appendix A) and time (Appendix B).

Care is learning to meet your spouse's most important emotional needs. When you achieve care, you deposit enough love units to create romantic love.

Time is the scheduling of undivided attention that is necessary to achieve care. Without time, it's impossible to meet you spouse's emotional needs.

With the tools I've given you, you can achieve something that only a small percentage have achieved in our generation: sustained romantic love. It takes thoughtfulness, but it's worth it!

Appendix A

How to Build Romantic Love With Care

When Sharon and Mike married, the most clearly understood part of their wedding vow was that they would care for each other throughout their lifetime. They understood that care means more than a feeling, it's a commitment to make every reasonable effort to meet each other's needs.

While they were still dating, Mike would tell Sharon that if she married him he'd make her the happiest woman in history. She'd be the center of his life, and his world would revolve around her. Sharon knew that if the marriage was to work she had to treat him the same way. She had to make him happy as well and make every effort to meet his needs.

While they each had the right intentions and the correct understanding of care as a marital commitment, they did not understand how difficult it would be to *learn* to care for each other. They both thought care was something you could decide to do, and once the decision was made, acts of care would be spontaneous.

But because their care for each other was not carefully planned, it fell far short of expectations. Both Sharon and Mike felt neglected.

Care is the *willingness* to change your own personal habits to meet the emotional needs of the person you have chosen to marry and then *making sure* that those habits are effective.

Care does not cause anyone to lose his or her identity or to become a robot. Our habits are very often developed through chance and are not necessarily a reflection of our character or our major goals in life. When we change them to accommodate our spouses' needs, we are actually controlling our behavior to fit our characters.

But the process of discarding old habits and developing new ones is difficult and stressful. This is one reason well-intentioned couples often fail in their efforts to learn more accommodating habits. It's not only difficult for us to change for our spouses, but it is also difficult to put our spouses through the stress of making changes to accommodate us.

Sharon and Mike thought they were compatible when they were married. They got along with each other extremely well and felt that they were made for each other. It did not occur to them that after marriage new marital needs would develop and prior acts of care would slowly fade away.

Care is more than learning to meet another's needs at a point in time and sustaining those habits; it also requires the willingness and ability to meet changing needs—adjusting to a moving target.

One of the more popular reasons for divorce today is that a husband and wife have "grown apart from each other." One of them may have completed an education, while the other did not. One may have developed new career interests, and the other did not join in those interests. Very often, children impact a couple's interests and send them in different directions.

I believe that one reason couples grow apart is that they fail to care for each other. Instead of learning how to meet each other's needs, couples assume that their instincts will carry them. Then when instinct seems to fail, they conclude that they must be incompatible. Growing apart means that a couple has not grown in compatibility. They have let nature take its course, and the new needs that are inevitable in marriage are left unmet, because no effort was made create new habits to meet them.

Extramarital affairs and multiple marriages represent one strategy in adjusting to the failure to create compatibility. Over a period of time, as needs change and a relationship falls apart, a new relationship may be created with another individual who, by chance, is prepared to meet those new needs.

If we were unable to adjust to each other's changes in life, then I suppose multiple marriages would be about the only solution to satisfactory relationships. But we have an enormous capacity for adjustment. Learning to meet each other's marital needs is far less complicated than going through the agonizing ritual of divorce and remarriage.

Step #1:
Discover Your Spouse's Most Important Needs

The first step in learning to care for your spouse is discovering his or her emotional needs and identifying the most important ones.

Men and women often have very different marital needs—especially the most important ones—and this makes discovering your spouse's needs complex and difficult. Because men try to meet needs most important to men and women try to meet needs most important to women, a couple can easily become confused and fail to meet each other's real needs.

When the best efforts of a man and woman go unappreciated and their own needs are not met besides, they often give up trying. If they had only directed their efforts in the right places, they would have been effective and appreciated.

My experience as a marriage counselor has pointed out ten of the most important emotional needs met in marriage. While all ten are important, five are of critical importance to most men, and the other five are of critical importance to most women. All these categories may not apply to your marriage, but they can help you begin a discussion with your spouse to identify the needs you should learn to meet.

A man's five most important needs in marriage tend to be:

1. *Sexual fulfillment*. His wife meets this need by becoming a terrific sexual partner. She studies her own sexual response to recognize and understand what brings out the best in her; then she shares this information with him, and together they learn to have a sexual relationship that both find repeatedly satisfying and enjoyable.
2. *Recreational companionship*. She develops an interest in the recreational activities he enjoys most and tries to become proficient at them. If she finds she cannot enjoy them, she encourages him to consider other activities that they can enjoy together. She becomes his favorite recreational companion, and he associates her with his most enjoyable moments of relaxation.
3. *Physical attractiveness*. She keeps herself physically fit with diet and exercise, and she wears her hair, makeup, and clothes in a way that he finds attractive and tasteful. He is attracted to her in private and proud of her in public.
4. *Domestic support*. She creates a home that offers him a refuge from the stresses of life. She manages household responsibilities in a way that encourages him to spend time at home enjoying his family.
5. *Admiration*. She understands and appreciates him more than anyone else. She reminds him of his value and achievements and helps him maintain self-confidence. She avoids criticizing him. She is proud of him, not out of duty, but from a profound respect for the man she chose to marry.

When a man is married to a woman who has learned to meet these needs, he'll find her irresistible. Love units are deposited into his love bank in such great numbers that he finds himself helplessly in love. That's because the fulfillment of these needs is essential to his happiness.

A woman's five most important needs in marriage tend to be:

1. *Affection.* Her husband tells her that he loves her with words, cards, flowers, gifts, and common courtesies. He hugs and kisses her many times each day, creating an environment of affection that clearly and repeatedly expresses his love for her.

2. *Conversation.* He sets aside time every day to talk to her. They may talk about events in their lives, their children, their feelings, or their plans. But whatever the topic, she enjoys the conversation because it is never judgmental, always informative and constructive. She talks to him as much as she would like, and he responds with interest. He is never too busy "to just talk."

3. *Honesty and openness.* He tells her everything about himself, leaving nothing out that might later surprise her. He describes his positive and negative feelings, events of his past, his daily schedule, and his plans for the future. He never leaves her with a false impression and is truthful about his thoughts, feelings, intentions, and behavior.

4. *Financial support.* He assumes the responsibility to house, feed, and clothe his family. If his income is insufficient to provide essential support, he resolves the problem by upgrading his skills to increase his salary. He does not work long hours, keeping himself from his wife and family, but is able to provide necessary support by working a forty- to forty-five-hour week. While he encourages his wife to pursue a career, he does not depend on her salary for family living expenses.

5. *Family commitment.* He commits sufficient time and energy to the moral and educational development of the children. He reads to them, engages in sports with them, and takes them on frequent outings. He reads books and attends lectures with her on the subject of child development so that they will do a good job training them. He and she discuss training methods and objectives until they agree. He does not proceed with any plan of training or discipline without her approval. He recognizes that his care of the children is critically important to her.

When a woman is married to a man who has learned to meet these needs, she'll find him irresistible. Love units are deposited in her Love

Bank in such great numbers that she finds herself helplessly in love. That's because the fulfillment of these needs is essential to her happiness.

Of course, *these categories do not apply to everyone*. Some men look at their list and throw two out to make room for two from my "woman's needs" list. Some women do the same. Belief that these categories are right for everyone is a big mistake!

I suggest these needs to help a couple start the process of identifying what they need the most in marriage. It is simply a way of helping you think through what makes you the happiest and most fulfilled. I also want couples to realize that what a man needs in marriage is usually quite different from what a woman needs. That makes the whole process of discovering your needs very personal; it's something you must do for yourself. Then you should explain your discovery to your spouse.

To make this process more accurate and reliable, I suggest that you first pick one need from the ten. Pretend that, in your marriage, it's all you'll get. The other nine needs will *not* be met. What need would you pick if you knew you would never get the rest? That's need number one.

Then do the same for need number two. If you will *not* get the other eight needs met, what two would you pick? Continue this process until you've picked five. Those are likely to be the needs you want your spouse to focus primary attention on.

Take a hard look at the needs you left behind. For example, if you did not include financial support, you should not expect your spouse to earn a dime! Is the one you chose more important to you? How about physical attractiveness? If your spouse neglects her appearance, gains weight, or dresses carelessly, what would your emotional reaction be?

Some of my clients tell me that all ten are of critical importance. They could not survive a marriage that neglected any of them. But my experience has shown me that if you can learn to do an outstanding job meeting only the *five* most important needs, you build more romantic love than if you do a mediocre job on all ten.

Most of us cannot be outstanding at everything; we must pick what is most important and concentrate on that. If you want to build romantic love with your spouse, meeting the *most important* emotional needs will do it.

Once you and your spouse have communicated your five most important emotional needs to each other, you're ready for the second step in learning to care for each other.

Step #2:
Learn to Meet Your Spouse's Most Important Needs

Learning to meet your spouse's five most important marital needs usually requires literally hundreds, maybe thousands of new habits. But the habits all eventually come together to form a whole. It's like learning a part in a play: You begin by learning each line, each motion, each cue, but eventually it comes together. It's naturally whole; it doesn't seem like hundreds of little pieces.

In order to build the myriad of habits necessary to meet your spouse's needs, you must have a carefully planned strategy. *His Needs, Her Needs* provides a few strategies for you to consider for each of the ten needs. But the need for financial support may require you to consult a vocational counselor. The need for sexual fulfillment may require help from a sex therapist.

However you develop it, a strategy—a plan—should be created that has a good chance of improving your ability to meet the needs your spouse identified as most important.

Once you implement your plan, you may need someone to report to for accountability. Your spouse is not a good choice, because your mentor may need to criticize your effort, and your spouse should not be forced into that role. A pastor or professional counselor may be better suited.

Finally, when you have completed your plan, your spouse is the ultimate evaluator of success. If, after all your effort, your spouse's needs are not being met, you must go back to the drawing board and plan a new strategy.

Honesty is essential at this stage of the program. If your plan does not meet your spouse's needs, it does neither of you any good to claim success.

But if you are successful, your spouse will tell you. You will see it in his or her eyes, and in the way your partner talks to you and responds to you. The "look of love" is unmistakable.

I view marriage as a profession. The skills I learn are designed to meet my spouse's most important emotional needs, and if I'm successful, she'll be in love with me. If she's not in love with me, I'm probably at fault and need to develop new skills.

Of course, if I'm not in love with her, and I've been honest about my feelings, it's her problem to solve.

As I've said earlier, *compatibility is created*. As a couple increases the number of habits that meet each other's marital needs, it improves their compatibility and their romantic love for each other.

We have such an opportunity in marriage to give each other exactly what we need. Many couples squander that. Don't let it happen to you!

Appendix B

How to Build Romantic Love With Time

Before Sharon and Mike were married, they spent the majority of their free time together. Her girlfriends knew that spending time with Mike was one of her highest priorities. Whenever they invited her somewhere, she would first check to see if she'd be missing an opportunity to be with Mike. Her girlfriends thought it was silly. On some occasions, she even broke dates with her girlfriends, if Mike had time to be with her.

Mike did the same. Soon he found that many of the things he enjoyed doing were abandoned because he was spending so much time with Sharon.

They would try to see each other on a daily basis. On days when they couldn't get together, they called each other and sometimes talked for hours.

The total amount of time spent with each other in an average week was fifteen to twenty-five hours. This included time on the telephone. But they weren't counting. They took whatever opportunities there were, and it turned out that way. When they were together, they tended to give each other quite a bit of attention.

After they were married, however, a change took place in the quality of their time together. While they were with each other much more often, they actually spent less time giving each other attention. Mike came home and watched television all evening, and sometimes he barely said a word to Sharon.

Before they were married, they scheduled time to be with each other. But after marriage, they felt that "dates" were not as important, so their time together was incidental to other priorities.

Courtship is a custom that gives people a chance to prove they can meet each other's marital needs. If enough love units are deposited, marriage usually follows. But without time, the test would fail, because it takes time to deposit enough love units to create romantic love.

As a reminder to couples who tend to let time slip away, I've suggested the following:

The Rule of Time

Give undivided attention to your spouse a minimum of fifteen hours each week, meeting his or her most important emotional needs.

One difficult aspect of marriage counseling is scheduling time for it. The counselor must work evenings and weekends because most couples will not give up work to make their appointments. Then you must schedule around a host of evening and weekend activities that take the husband and wife in opposite directions.

Another difficult aspect of marriage counseling is arranging time for the couple to be together to carry out their first assignment. You see, they think that a counselor will solve their problems with a weekly conversation in his office. It doesn't occur to them that what they do after they leave the office saves their marriage. To accomplish anything, they must reserve time. You should see some of the pained expressions. ("We don't have *time* to be alone together. Think of something else we can do.")

Eventually they get the point. And little by little they rearrange their lives to include each other.

It's incredible how many couples have tried to talk me out of this rule. They begin by trying to convince me that it's impossible. Then they go on to the argument that it's impractical. Then they try to show me that it's impractical for *them*. But in the end, they usually agree that without time they cannot possibly achieve romantic love.

To help me explain how the rule of time is to be applied in marriage, I've broken it down into three parts: Privacy, objectives, and amount.

> **1.** *Privacy***: The time you plan to be together should not include children, relatives, or friends. Establish privacy so that you are able to give each other undivided attention.**

Why be alone? Because when you're alone as a couple, you have an opportunity to deposit many more love units in each other's Love Bank. When you're with others, everyone gets a little credit. Without privacy, romance in marriage simply comes to a halt.

First, I recommend that couples learn to be without their children during these fifteen hours. I'm amazed at how difficult an assignment that is for some people. They don't regard their children as company! To them, an evening with their children is *privacy*. They think that all it prevents is lovemaking, and they can do that after they go to bed. But I think it prevents much more than that: It keeps them from focusing attention on each other, something desperately needed in marriage.

Second, I recommend that they learn not to include friends and relatives during the fifteen hours. In many cases, there's no time left over for friends and relatives. If that's the case, you're too busy, but at least you haven't sacrificed romance.

Third, I teach couples what giving undivided attention means. Remember, it's what you did when you were dating. There's no way you would have married if you had ignored each other on dates. You looked at each other when you were talking; you were interested in the conversation; and there was little to distract you. You must to the same things now.

When you see a movie, the time watching doesn't count, because you're not giving each other undivided attention. Television is the same. So are sporting events. I want you to engage in these recreational activities, but the time that I'm talking about is to be very clearly defined: It's the time you pay close attention to each other.

Now that you're alone with each other, what should you do with this time? The second part of this rule helps me explain the answer to that question.

2. *Objectives*. **During this time, create activities that will meet your most important marital needs: Affection, sexual fulfillment, conversation, and recreational companionship.**

Romance for most men is sex and recreation; for women it's affection and conversation. When all four come together, men and women alike call it romance. That makes these categories somewhat inseparable. My advice is to combine them all, if you can, whenever you're alone with each other. That's what people do when they write romantic novels or are having an affair. Why limit romance to novels and affairs?

Now for the final part of this rule. How *much* time do you need?

3. *Amount*: **Choose a number of hours that reflects the quality of your marriage. If your marriage is satisfying to you and your spouse, plan fifteen hours. But if you suffer marital dissatisfaction, plan thirty hours each week or more, until marital satisfaction is achieved. Keep a permanent record of your time together.**

How much time do you need to sustain romance? Believe it or not, there really is an answer to this question, and it depends on the health of a marriage. If a couple is deeply in love with each other and finds that their marital needs are being met, I have found that about fifteen hours each week of undivided attention is usually enough to sustain a romantic marriage. It is probably the least amount of time necessary.

When a marriage is this healthy, it's either a new marriage or the couple has already been spending fifteen hours a week alone with each other. When I apply the fifteen-hour principle to new marriages, I usually recommend that the time be evenly distributed through the week, two to three hours each day. When time must be bunched up, all hours on the weekend, good results are not as predictable. People seem to need intimacy almost on a daily basis.

For couples on the verge of divorce or entangled in an affair, I recommend much more time. In some cases, I have advised couples to take a leave of absence from work and other responsibilities, go on a vacation, and spend the entire time restoring intimacy that was lost over the years. In many cases, two or three weeks of undivided attention bring them to a point where they begin to consider remaining married. I'm usually counseling them long-distance during this time.

The vacation doesn't usually build enough love units to re-create the feeling of love. But the feeling of hatred is reduced and sometimes eliminated. Remember, in bad marriages, Love Busters have created Love Bank balances that are in the *red*. Negative accounts must first be brought to zero before positive accounts can be built. These vacations are designed to speed up the love unit deposits before divorce sinks the ship.

When marriages are unhealthy but not on the verge of divorce, I recommend an intermediate amount of time together, somewhere between twenty and thirty hours a week. Without the crisis of divorce at hand, I usually have great difficulty talking people into being alone this long.

It's always been a mystery to me how workaholic businessmen find time to have an affair. The man who can't be home for dinner is scheduling mid-afternoon adventures three times a week. How does he get his work done? The answer, of course, is that he had the time all along. It was simply a matter of priorities. He could just as easily have taken time to be with his wife. Then he would have been madly in love with her instead of his secretary.

The reason I have so much difficulty getting these couples to spend time alone together is that they're not in love. Their relationship doesn't do anything for them, and the time spent together seems a total waste at first. But with that time they can learn to re-create the romantic experiences that first brought them together in a love relationship. Without that time, they have little hope of restoring the love they once had for each other.

Whether your marriage needs fifteen hours a week or more than that, remember that the time spent is only equivalent to a part-time job. It isn't time you don't have; it's time you've filled with something less important.

To help couples get into the habit of scheduling time alone, I have encouraged them to make a chart, measuring the number of hours alone each week. Each person independently estimates the time actually spent giving undivided attention, and the number on the chart should be the lower of the two estimates.

This graph becomes an excellent predictor of marital fulfillment. It's like the Leading Index of Economic Indicators for marital health. During periods when a couple spends large numbers of hours alone together, they can look forward in future months to a very warm and intimate love relationship. But when the chart shows that very few hours have been spent together, in the months ahead the couple can expect to find themselves arguing more often and feeling less fulfilled.

I also encourage both husband and wife to carry an appointment book. Here they write down the time they've set aside to be with each other. While I'm counseling them, I make certain that they keep the dates they set for each other and that they are always recorded.

Since we are creatures of habit, I recommend that the fifteen hours spent alone each week be repeated if at all possible. For example,

Monday, 8:00–10:00 P.M., Tuesday 8:00–10:00 P.M., Wednesday, 8:00–10:00 P.M., Friday 6:00–10:00 P.M., Saturday 12:00–5:00 P.M., and Sunday 6:00–10:00 P.M. If you keep that schedule every week, it will be easier to follow the Rule of Time than if you change it every week.

Remember, the total amount of time you spend together doesn't necessarily affect the way you feel about each other in the week that the time was spent. It has more effect on the way you're *going to feel* about each other in future weeks. You're building Love Bank accounts when you spend time together, and the account must build before you feel the effect.

From my perspective as a marriage counselor, the time you spend alone with each other are the most valuable moments of your week. It's the time when you are depositing the most love units and ensuring romantic love for your marriage.

Dr. Willard F. Harley, Jr., is a clinical psychologist and marriage and family therapist. He has over 25 years experience in marriage counseling and owns and directs a network of mental health clinics in Minnesota. Dr. Harley's wife, Joyce, is a Christian radio personality, recording artist, and directs several ministries. They are the parents of two married children and have two grandchildren. Their home is in White Bear Lake, Minnesota.